MW01289504

Acclaim for The Essential Fundraising Guide for K-12...

"THERE IS LIKELY NO ONE IN THE COUNTRY WHO KNOWS MORE ABOUT FUNDRAISING FOR PUBLIC SCHOOLS THAN STAN LEVENSON."

He puts 40 years of hands-on experience into a remarkable book. *The Essential Fundraising Guide for K-12 Schools* is absolute must reading— for classroom teachers, school administrators, and volunteers. There's nothing else like it. It takes you by the hand and leads you through every step in a school's fundraising program. It is fail-proof in building a successful design that ensures you of raising a great deal of money. There are 350 Links. The Blogs and Bibliographies alone are worth the price of the book. It's a feast of helpful tips and information. Dr. Levenson says, "There is no better cause than public education." He makes this come alive in his book.

Jerold Panas, Best Selling Author and Founding Partner of Jerold Panas, Linzy & Partners

Stan Levenson thought of everything. You're in good hands. One book, and you'll know exactly how to succeed in the savagely competitive education grants arena.

Tom Ahern, Author, *Making Money With Donor Newsletters; How to Write Fundraising Materials that Raise More Money; and Seeing Through a Donor's Eyes.*

The Essential Fundraising Guide for K-12 Schools is a great resource for the first-time and veteran fundraiser alike. Whether you're looking for donors to fund a classroom project, or launching a capital campaign to build a new facility, Stan offers dozens of practical tips and know-how to make the most of your efforts.

Charles Best, CEO DonorsChoose.org

Legendary, fundraising and "friendraising" guru, Stan Levenson, has done it again! He's created another terrific tool to boost both awareness and skills in the competitive arena of school fundraising. The best school leaders and community advocates are always seeking ways to preserve and enhance educational quality for all children by boosting resources and winning new donors. This book unlocks a treasure-trove of proven best practices for creating a comprehensive school fundraising program and should be on the desk of every school development officer and savvy school leader.

Howie Schaffer, President, Bonanza Communications, Founding Editor, PEN Weekly NewsBlast

Stan has hit it out of the park again! His book puts in one place all the information that preK-12 staff would need, no matter the demographics of their campus/school, methods to obtain additional resources to meet their stakeholders' needs. This is a book that both the first time "grant writer" and the twenty-year expert can benefit from reading.

Gary Lee Frye, Ed.D. GPC, Homeless Liaison / Grant Writer, Lubbock-Cooper ISD Executive Director for Llano Estacado Rural Communities Foundation. Lubbock, TX

Stan has been a real encouragement to me both personally and professionally through his books. As founder and executive director of the National School Foundation Association I sold his books both from our website and our national conferences as a trusted fundraising guide to our members. Thanks Stan for another great resource for the over 5,000 K-12 Education Foundation leaders in the US seeking to offer additional educational opportunities to their partnering schools.

Jim Collogan, President, ASA Strategic Funding

Updated and Revised 2019

The Essential Fundraising Guide for K-12 Schools

(A 1-Hour Book With More Than 350 Links)

Stan Levenson, Ph.D.

Author's Note: We're working to maintain all of the relevant links—please let me know if you find any dead or broken links.

Updated and Revised 2019

The Essential Fundraising Guide for K-12 Schools

(A 1-Hour Book With More Than 350 Links)

Stan Levenson, Ph.D.

Contents

9

Chapter 4

Chapter 5

Chapter 6

Chapter 7

Chapter 8

Chapter 9

Chapter 10
Creating & Maintaining School and District 501(c)(3) Foundations _____ **113**

Chapter 11
Staff Development, Consultant Services and Recruitment _____ **117**

Chapter 12
Professional Publications _____ **121**

Chapter 13
Professional Associations _____ **123**

Chapter 14

Introduction

This revised and updated second edition of *The Essential Fundraising Guide for K-12 Schools: A 1-Hour Book With More Than 350 Links* has dozens of new links to give teachers, principals, parents, superintendents, philanthropists, school board members and school foundation board members easy access to top funding resources and opportunities.

KEY FEATURES OF THE SECOND EDITION

- New and updated funding resources and links.

- Detailed program information and assistance for DonorsChoose.org, the largest mini-grant program in the world for public school teachers.

- A brand new section on funding needs and opportunities for Early Childhood Education.

- An updated discussion on trends in Naming Rights for public schools and school districts including the identification of additional schools and districts that have negotiated Naming Rights.

- Job description for new position, Director of Alumni Relations added to Development Office Staff.

- Updated bibliography and Others

Many of you know that I have been involved in fundraising in K-12 public schools for more than 45 years. In all the years that I have been active, I continue to encounter the need for outside funding for the public schools. Every political leader says education is their #1 priority. Yet the relentless slashing of school budgets tells a truer story of the gap between talk and walk when it comes to school funding. Many public schools struggling to balance budgets have fired teachers, slashed course offerings, and charged fees to students for riding the bus, singing in the chorus, belonging to clubs, or participating on sports teams. This is not the American way! Your feedback is important to me. Please keep in touch via Twitter @StanLevenson and good luck along the way.

Chapter 1

Grants for Teachers and Schools

K-12 classroom teachers are busy people. They need all the help they can get. I know this as a fact. I've been there, done that. My wife has been a teacher for many years. My daughter-in-law is a teacher. It's a daunting task! Good teachers are constantly dipping into their wallets to pay for paper, pencils, pens, computers and other necessities not available in today's schools. How can classroom teachers find funding for some of the basic necessities they need in their classrooms today? Also, how can classroom teachers find monies for some of the things that have been eliminated at their schools like music, art, P.E. foreign languages, and field trips? You've come to the right place!

This chapter will lead you in the right direction and alleviate some of the budget strains that you face each and every day. Take a look below and feast your eyes on sites like DonorsChoose.org, Grants Alert, Education World Grants Center, The Foundation Center, eSchool News, and others.

DONORSCHOOSE.ORG

In 2000, Charles Best, a New York City public school teacher, spent a lot of time in the teacher's lunchroom, talking with his fellow teachers about the books they wanted their students to read, the art projects they wanted them to engage in, and the field trips they wanted their students to take. They didn't have the funding to do these things, so Best founded DonorsChoose.org out of his classroom. In 2007, this nonprofit organization expanded to serve every public school teacher in the United States, and today it is one of the most successful fundraising programs in the country.

HOW IT WORKS: Public school teachers from every corner of America post short classroom project requests on DonorsChoose.org. Requests range from pencils for a poetry-writing unit, to violins for a school recital, to microscope slides for a biology class. Individuals can browse through the requests and give any amount online to the project that inspires them. Once a project reaches its funding goal, DonorsChoose.org sends the materials to the school. All donors hear back from the classroom they supported with thank-you notes and photos. At DonorsChoose.org, anyone can give as little as $1 and get the same level of choice, transparency, and feedback that is traditionally reserved for someone who gives millions. They call it "citizen philanthropy."

I became aware of DonorsChoose.org when they first started operating in New York City in 2000. Their motto was "Teachers Ask, You Choose." This approach appealed to me so much that I personally became involved as a donor. The first project I funded was a second-grade reading project in the Bronx. They took my personal info and money online with my credit card. It was as simple as paying for almost anything online. The staff provided the classroom teacher with my name and also purchased the materials for her to implement the project. I got immediate positive feedback from the teacher and the kids, as they were in touch with me via the DonorsChoose.org website and thanked me profusely. I was also able to communicate with the kids via the teacher online. As a follow-up, I received wonderful thank-you notes with photos from the kids in the mail. I became so excited about DonorsChoose.org that I started mentioning it in my writings and talks and was hopeful that the idea would spread across the country. I continue to fund projects and encourage others to do so as well.

Since 2000, the DonorsChoose.org community of more than 3.6 million donors and dozens of corporate and foundation partners have channeled more than $790 million into classrooms in need and benefited more than 32.8 million students in all 50 states and the District of Columbia, including public charter schools. It is interesting to note that at this time 81% of all public school teachers have posted a project on this site. You too, can post a project. Below is the info you need to get started. You won't be sorry!

Personal Recommendations Concerning Getting Funded on DonorsChoose.org

I have helped hundreds of teachers get their projects fully funded on DonorsChoose.org via my Twitter Account. I have also given thousands of dollars to many teachers' projects. While I can't guarantee that my recommendations work 100% of the time, here they are:

1. Do not ask for thousands of dollars in funding. This is a mini-grant program.

2. If your project is over $1,000, break you project down into two smaller projects.

3. For large requests, go to my list of 125 Foundations and Corporations Interested in Giving to the Public Schools in Chapter 5.

4. Utilize Twitter to assist in having people get to know you. Follow people who are interested in helping you get funded and give monies themselves.

5. Make certain to tell about yourself on your Twitter Introductory Page. e.g. Are you a teacher? Where? Grade(s)? Interests? Other Interests? Also, provide a photo.

GET STARTED RIGHT NOW WITH DONORSCHOOSE.ORG

http://www.donorschoose.org/teachers

MORE GRANTS FOR TEACHERS AND SCHOOLS

In addition to DonorsChoose.org, there are many more funding opportunities for individual classroom teachers, schools, and school districts. The following links will save you time and energy and familiarize you with what's out there.

Grants Alert
http://www.GrantsAlert.com

Education World (Grants Center)
http://www.educationworld.com/a_ admin/archives/grants.shtml

The Foundation Center
http://www.foundationcenter.org

Grant Space
http://grantspace.org/Subjects/education

eSchool News
http://www.eschoolnews.com/funding/

Requests For Proposals (RFPs)
http://foundationcenter.org/pnd/rfp/

The School Funding Center
https://www.schoolfundingcenter.info/index.aspx

Grantmakers for Education
http://www.edfunders.org/

Philanthropy Roundtable
http://www.philanthropyroundtable.org/
home/programs/k-12-education ·

Edutopia- Grant Announcements and Resources
https://www.edutopia.org/topic/fundraising-supplies

National PTA and Schwan's Home Service
https://www.pta.org/home/run-your-pta/Awards-Grants

The Scholastic Funding Connection
http://teacher.scholastic.com/products/nclb/

Grant Gopher
https://www.grantgopher.com/

Technology Grants and Gifts
http://www.techsoup.org/joining-techsoup

Box Tops for Education
http://www.boxtops4education.com/home

Campbell's Soup Labels
   https://www.campbellsoupcompany.com/
   about-campbell/corporate-responsibility/
   campbell-soup-foundation/

Scholastic Book Clubs
   https://clubs2.scholastic.com/
   contests-and-programs.html

Classwish
   http://classwish.org/

Adopt-A-Classroom
   http://www.adoptaclassroom.org/

Supply Our Schools
   http://www.nea.org/tools/lessons/
   supply-our-schools.html

All For Schools
   https://all4schools.org/

Digital Wish
   http://www.digitalwish.com/dw/digitalwish/home

Book Mentors
   http://www.bookmentors.org/

First Book
   http://www.firstbook.org/

National Association of Independent Schools
   http://www.nais.org/search/?mssearch=fundraising

Fundraising Ideas
   http://www.fundraising-ideas.org/DIY/

Chapter 2

Grant Writing From Mini-Grants to Major Grants

I have written a lot of grants in my 45 years in education. Most of the grants were funded. Others weren't worth a plug nickel. I will focus on teaching you how to write mini-grants as well as major grants and will also provide you with information to garner as many grants as you need for your classroom, school, or district. The things that you will learn along the way will encourage funders to part with their money on your behalf. Once you learn how to write a mini-grant, it will be that much easier to write major grants. Just add a few more zeros in your budget and follow the directions to a tee, and you will have a major grant.

I think of a mini-grant as any grant under $5,000, but you can use your own definition. Many schools, foundations, and corporations have mini-grant programs. DonorsChoose. org is a mini-grant program. Accessing the websites cited in this book, as well as funding agencies in your city, county, and state, will alert you to the mini-grant funding opportunities that are out there for the asking. For major grant opportunities, expand your search by going to the sites mentioned in this book and elsewhere. When you start applying for major grants and gifts, you will be competing with full-time grant writers, consultants, and specialists, and the chances of getting funded become slimmer.

If you do not get funded the first or second time you apply for a mini-grant, do not get discouraged. There are usually many more applicants than there are funds for projects. Keep honing your skills, and the monies will start to flow in.

GETTING STARTED

Regardless of the size of the grant opportunity, there are six basic components to any grant application. These are:

1. NEEDS ASSESSMENT. This analyzes the extent of the problem and the conditions you wish to change. The statement of the problem or need represents the reason for your proposal.

2. GOALS. Goals are general in nature, broad-based, and overarching. They summarize what you want to accomplish in your grant application. It is recommended that you state just one or two goals in your application.

3. OBJECTIVES. When writing the objectives for your project, divide them into program objectives and process objectives. Program objectives specify the outcomes of your project—the end product. These should be measurable and time-specific and become the criteria by which your program will be evaluated. Process objectives are also measurable and are written to assure that the program objectives are carried out. Here are examples of each:

- **PROGRAM OBJECTIVE:** At the conclusion of the project period, at least 80 percent of the target students will gain at least one month academically for each month of instruction in reading vocabulary and reading comprehension, as measured by a standardized test selected by the school or district.

- **PROCESS OBJECTIVE**: At the conclusion of the project period, at least 80 percent of the target students will have visited the school library at least once a week to select books for leisure-time reading, as measured by records kept by the school librarian.

4. ACTIVITIES. The activities (methods) section of your application will explain in detail how you are going to achieve the desired outcomes stated in your objectives. Activities explain what will be done, who will do it, and when it will get done. Several activities are presented for each objective. The activities section should flow smoothly from the needs statement and the program objectives.

5. EVALUATION SPECIFICATIONS. This part of your application should help the funding agency determine the extent to which the objectives of your project will be met and the activities carried out. Be certain to describe your evaluation plan as clearly and succinctly as you can. First, take a look at the overall project. Study the goals, objectives, and activities. If the objectives written are truly measurable, then it should not be difficult to evaluate each objective. The objectives should have built-in evaluation criteria. (See Objectives, above.)

6. BUDGET. The budget that you present to the funding agency delineates the costs involved in carrying out your project and expresses what you are trying to accomplish. It is important that you prepare this section carefully because it has an impact upon your credibility with the funding agency. You might want to consult with your principal or district business manager on this section as you break out your costs. A number of funding agencies have their own budget page that they want you to complete. Others ask you to prepare your own budget page. For a mini-grant, the following budget categories will suffice for most funding agencies:

Project Budget

1. Personnel
2. Fringe Benefits
3. Travel
4. Equipment
5. Supplies
6. Contractual
7. Other
8. Total Costs

Once you learn how to write a mini-grant, you are well on your way to writing other successful grant applications, including major grants. The ideas presented will assist in making this a reality.

FEDERAL AND STATE GRANTS

In my previous fundraising books and articles in professional journals I spent a lot of time talking about how to write both federal and state grant applications and provided examples for each. However, I now believe that most school districts are experienced at writing these applications and do not need as much assistance as they did in the past. I do, however, want to emphasize that when you write a federal or state grant you are competing with the big boys and girls on the block, and in most instances, large city school districts. So, if you are not in this category, it will be a lot more fruitful to go to corporations and foundations for funding, or to individuals in your communities. I also want to point out that if you do plan to go after federal and state grants, following my suggestions above will assist you in your quest for these monies. Below you will find a comprehensive array of links to federal and state funding opportunities that will make your job easier, and assist in bringing in more funding than you ever imagined.

GOVERNMENT GRANT OPPORTUNITIES

U.S. Department of Education
   http://www2.ed.gov/fund/grants-apply.html

U.S. Government Grants
   http://www.grants.gov/web/grants/search-grants.html

Grants.gov
   http://www.grants.gov

Federal Funding Tools and Links (Michigan State University)
   http://staff.lib.msu.edu/harris23/grants/federal.htm

Thompson Information Services
   http://grants.thompson.com/

Federal Funding Links (York College)
https://www.york.cuny.edu/finaid/
grants-loans-scholarships

Federal Grant Reform
http://tgci.com/blog/2013/12/federal-grant-reform-here

Office of Juvenile Justice and Delinquency Prevention
http://web.archive.org/web/20001203115500/

http://ojjdp.ncjrs.org/grants/grants.html

GRANT ANNOUNCEMENTS

Grants Alert
http://www.grantsalert.com/grant-writers

Grant Station
https://www.grantstation.com/

The Grantsmanship Center
http://tgci.com/funding-sources

e-School News
http://www.eschoolnews.com/?s=Funding

Insight Grants Development
http://insightgrants.com/findgrants/

GRANT WRITING TRAINING

The Grantsmanship Center
http://www.tgci.com

The Foundation Center
   http://www.foundationcenter.org

Grant Writing Boot Camp
   https://grantspace.org/training/courses/
   proposal-writing-boot-camp/

Grant Writing USA
   http://www.grantwritingUSA.com/

GRANT WRITING CONSULTANTS (K-12)

There are a number of outstanding grant writing consultants for K-12 located across the United States. Below you will find a "starter list." It is recommended that you study these links and interview those consultants that interest you. I have mentioned elsewhere in my writing that it is not a good idea to employ outside consultants to write grants on a percentage basis. It is in your best interest as a school, district, or foundation to avoid this kind of an arrangement. Most experienced, reliable consultants will not work this way. Also, some school districts are paying a flat fee to grant writing consultants at this time based upon the size and scope of the grant. This appears to meet the needs of school districts and consultants. See below.

Grant Professionals Association
   https://www.grantprofessionals.org/
   AF_ConsultantDirectory.asp

Grants Alert
   https://grantsalert.com/grant-writers/

Grant Writing Consultants, Michigan State University, Jon Harrison
   http://staff.lib.msu.edu/harris23/grants/fraisers.htm

Insight Grants Development
  http://insightgrants.com

Educational Resource Consultants (ERC)
  https://www.ercdata.com/grantwriting

Carol F. Inman
  http://nationalgrantwriter.com/

Jan-Mitchell Johnson
  http://grantsformation.com/

Seliger + Associates
  http://www.seliger.com/

Jay Katz
  https://grantswest.com/

Nikki Kirk
  http://www.simplegrantresearch.info/

Kassie Clarke
  ttp://www.grant-expectations.com/

Marcie Wagner
  http://www.wagnerfundraising.com/

Shelley Maberry
  http://www.maberryconsulting.com/

Innovative Ideas for Grants

The George Lucas Educational Foundation (GLEF)
http://www.edutopia.org/mission-vision

Barrel of Monkeys
http://www.barrelofmonkeys.org

Grant Writing Books
http://www.amazon.com/s/ref=nb_sb_
noss_1?url=search-alias%3Dstripbooks&field-
keywords=Grant+Writing+Books

http://staff.lib.msu.edu/harris23/grants/4edfrais.htm

Chapter 3

Corporate and Foundation Grants

CORPORATE GIVING

Corporations provide support to nonprofit organizations, including schools, through their own private foundations, direct-giving programs, or both. These separate legal entities maintain close ties with their parent organizations, and their giving philosophies usually mirror company priorities and interests. Corporate foundations are required to follow the laws and regulations governing private foundations, including filing an annual Form 990-PF with the Internal Revenue Service. The 990-PF provides a complete grants list, the names of the foundation's trustees and officers, and other relevant information.

Having access to 990-PFs will assist you in determining the giving trends of a particular foundation as well as the size of the grants made and other vital data. Fortunately, 990-PFs are public records, and you can access these documents through the Foundation Center and tax returns for foundations in state attorneys general offices. For additional information on accessing 990-PF Forms go to: http://foundationcenter.org/

findfunders/990finder/

In addition to corporate foundations, corporations are also involved in direct-giving programs. These giving programs are not separately incorporated and the IRS does not require the corporation to adhere to private foundation laws or regulations, including the filing of Form 990-PF. Corporations are allowed to deduct up to 10 percent of their pre-tax income for charitable purposes.

In my work in the public schools, I have discovered that corporations typically contribute in those communities where their employees live and work. I have also discovered that corporations are interested in forming partnerships with the schools and typically contribute dollars, equipment, and resource personnel to the schools. Some corporations have mini-grant programs. Others have mentoring and volunteer programs for kids and schools. Become familiar with all the corporations located in or near your school or school district and involve and welcome them in your schools. Invite corporate CEOs to become members of your foundation board or your Board of Trustees. Many of the people working at these corporations have kids or grandkids attending your schools. They want to contribute to your cause. Ask for their help!

INDEPENDENT FOUNDATIONS

Independent (private) foundations are nongovernmental, usually have a principal fund or endowment, are managed by a board of trustees and directors, and give cash and non-cash gifts to the schools. America's 1,000 leading private foundations have given annually to colleges, universities, nonprofit organizations, and the schools. They typically support charitable, educational, religious, and other causes that serve the public good.

Independent foundations are interested in funding "excellence" and innovation in the public schools. They typically have not been interested in compensatory education or remedial types of programs, although some foundations do support these efforts. Independent foundations are concerned with bringing about change in a positive manner or in enhancing and supplementing outstanding existing programs. Some foundations support math, science, and the environment, while others are interested in music, art, and dance. Certain foundations give preference to computer technology and literacy, while still others are interested in health education, parent education, and staff development. Some independent foundations support capital equipment, however, only insofar as the equipment is directly related to a clear vision and an overall program plan.

Most recently, a number of independent foundations have become interested in the charter school movement and have given millions of dollars to the schools. As such, many charter schools have more dollars per child behind them. What this suggests is that with more dollars behind each child, and with more innovative programming, the public schools can and will succeed. I am very interested in seeing more private and public dollars flow to the public schools just like at the public colleges and universities.

COMMUNITY FOUNDATIONS

There are more than 700 community foundations across the United States. These foundations are usually made up of individuals, businesses, and organizations located in specific communities or regions. Within certain parameters, anyone can be a donor to a community foundation. Donors can give cash, stock, bonds, real estate, and other assets. These gifts can usually be made within the lifetime of the donors or through their estates, with the donors receiving maximum tax benefits.

There are community foundations located in every state in the United States. Grants from these foundations help to support charitable groups and programs working to improve the quality of life within a specific community or region. Over the past several years, I have observed community foundations become more interested in the public schools. Competitive grant programs such as teachers' funds to assist classroom teachers with mini-grants have been established. I have been fortunate to work with the San Diego Community Foundation as Chairperson of the Teacher Fund Committee. Since 1995, the Teacher Fund Committee has distributed more than $1 million in teacher mini-grants.

Other types of innovative grants are also being made to schools by community foundations to provide funding for programs that improve teaching and learning in the classroom. These foundations are sprouting up all over the country. They are a good source of funding for teachers, schools, and school districts. Take the time to locate the community foundations in your area of the country and get to know the people who are responsible for awarding grants and gifts.

PRO BONO AND IN-KIND GIFTS

There are many opportunities for schools and school districts to obtain pro bono and in-kind gifts from corporations and foundations in your community. Study the links below and make personal contacts for assistance.

http://www.amazon.com/Powered-Pro-Bono-Step-Step/dp/1118140958

https://grantspace.org/resources/
knowledge-base/in-kind-gifts/

http://www.raise-funds.com/in-kind-gifts-
how-to-acknowledge-and-recognize-them/

REQUESTS FOR PROPOSALS (RFPS)

Some corporations and foundations announce requests for proposals on their websites, in newsletters, and in publications. By announcing an RFP, the funding agency is pinpointing and targeting its monies in specific interest areas. To some school districts, this is positive in that they will receive applications that respond to a specific need or concern of the funding agency. As a school or school district, there are advantages and disadvantages in responding to an RFP. The first advantage is that you already know what the foundation is interested in by the materials it provides in the RFP package. Second, you will probably be told for what size grant to apply and how many grants will get funded. One of the major disadvantages of responding to an RFP is that your focus will be narrowed down to the specific interest area of the funding agency. Of course, if your interests match the funding agency's interest area, this is not a problem. Another disadvantage is that you will probably have more competition in obtaining the grant if the foundation announces it to the world via its website and through other publications. More people generally respond to an RFP than make individual contacts with foundations. I would recommend that if you do respond to an RFP, use the same grant writing techniques discussed in this book.

While I don't want to leave you with the impression that it is easy to obtain monies from corporations and foundations,

I do want to point out that in my experience working in the public schools, I found that obtaining corporate and foundation funding was less demanding than obtaining funding from government grants. I have also discovered that obtaining these grants takes more nurturing and personal contact. Some people like this, while others do not.

Following in chapter 4 is a 15-step strategy for winning corporate and foundation funding for your school or district. It is based upon my experience working in the public schools.

Chapter 4

15-Step Strategy for Winning Corporate and Foundation Grants

Below is an 15-step strategy for winning corporate and foundation funding for K-12 schools. These strategies have proven successful in my work in the schools, and they should be helpful and practical for you as you think about and apply for funding from corporations and foundations.

STEP 1. Have an innovative idea and vision in mind. Collaborate with a team of 2 to 5 people who share your passion. Obtain administrative support for your idea. Ask for release time for teachers to write the grant application if funds are available.

STEP 2. Begin to do prospect research by becoming familiar with corporate and foundation funding agencies in your local area, the state, and the nation that are interested in funding K-12 education programs. It is usually easier to obtain monies from local and statewide foundations and corporations rather than national foundations that traditionally fund projects having national implications and significance. However, if your project meets the criteria of any of the national foundations, go for it.

STEP 3. Access the Foundation Center website at http://fdncenter.org to locate corporations and foundations in your area, including community foundations that might be interested in making grants to the schools. The Foundation Center website, which is free, is loaded with worthwhile information for people doing basic research on corporate and foundation giving. This database is also available free through the Foundation Center's main cooperating collections located in New York City, Washington, DC, Atlanta, Cleveland, and San Francisco, and in smaller cooperating collections located all across the United States. You can find out where these locations are by accessing http://fdncenter.org/collections/index.html. Also, study the links in this book carefully. They are a treasure trove and it's all here for you in one place.

STEP 4. Once you have completed the prospect research phase, you are now ready to request the most recent information, yearbooks, and applications from the corporations and foundations that are potential funding sources for your school or district. You can usually find this info online. In larger school districts or county school offices where corporate and foundation files are kept up to date, contact the person who is responsible for fundraising and ask for assistance. Also, go to the vast array of links supplied in this book.

STEP 5. Make multiple copies of relevant applications and materials, and read and study them carefully. Reread several times. Check to see if there are any deadline dates of which you need to be aware. Find out how many public school projects were funded previously, including the amounts of funding. Pinpoint the deadline dates on your calendar.

STEP 6. Telephone the program officer at the foundation or corporation to discuss your ideas and to begin the "nurturing process." If you already know the program officer this is a positive. Make certain that you are thoroughly familiar with your project and that you are able to discuss it with clarity, conviction, and strength. Also, be prepared to respond to any questions or concerns of the program officer and incorporate any relevant suggestions for improvement. For example, one question that is often asked is "How are you planning to evaluate this project?" If it appears that the program officer is interested in your project and that monies are available to meet your needs based upon your prospect research, ask for an appointment to visit the foundation with your site or district-level administrator. In instances where you are requesting a considerable amount of money, it is recommended that you invite your superintendent of schools and a board member to join you in meeting with the chief operating officer of the foundation. This person-to-person contact, especially with the heads of both organizations, could do wonders for your corporate and foundation fundraising effort. In fact, this approach is used on a continuing basis by private schools, colleges, universities, and nonprofit organizations. College and university presidents are "on the road" on a continuing basis soliciting funds. Why can't superintendents of schools make this part of their job description?

STEP 7. If you are unable to visit the funding agency, invite the program officer of the agency and other staff members to visit you. If there appears to be no interest in any visitations or in having you submit an application, go on to another funding agency with your ideas.

STEP 8. If you are fortunate enough to have the funding agency indicate that it would like to make a site visit, then you are on the right track for getting funded. This is one of the key indicators that the agency is interested in your project. Sometimes a site visit might not be scheduled until after you submit an application. In either case, you have good reason to get a little excited. Determine how much time the program officer will spend in the district, including arrival and departure times. Prepare carefully for the visit. Include an agenda that will be mailed out or e-mailed to the visitor and other invited guests ahead of time. Include in the agenda the district's demographics, the case for support, and the schedule for the day. Invite key people to the entrance and exit meetings, including the superintendent, principal(s), one or two board members, and representative parents and teachers.

STEP 9. Meet the program officer at the airport, if this person is arriving by plane. Provide for food, snacks, lunch, and lodging, if appropriate. Your goal is to impress the visitor with your school or school district and proposed project.

STEP 10. Upon arrival at the entrance meeting, which could take place at the district office or at a school site, introduce the program officer and other visitors to each person at the meeting, and then proceed to review the day's activities with everyone.

STEP 11. Follow your time schedule and agenda very carefully, leaving time for classroom visits and observations (if appropriate), lunch, follow-up, and the scheduled exit meeting.

STEP 12. The same people who were invited to the entrance meeting should be invited to the exit meeting. The goal of the exit meeting is to ascertain whether the program officer is impressed with what was seen and whether the program officer is ready to recommend the district for funding. In a number of instances, I have witnessed program officers at exit meetings tell district officials that they were so impressed with what they had seen that they were prepared to recommend the district for funding. They went on further to request that the district put together an application of three to five pages asking for a given amount of dollars. In instances when the program officer does not disclose this information to the group, I believe it would be appropriate to ask the following questions: "What impressed you the most about your visit today?" "Do you have any suggestions for improvement?" "Are you thinking about recommending us for funding?" "How much funding should we be requesting?" Note: Have a carefully prepared budget available that is categorized and well thought out. Also indicate how much the district is going to contribute to the project. You can use "in-kind" contributions for this purpose, such as staff assigned to coordinate and facilitate the project, facilities that you will be using, utility and custodial costs, and costs for materials and equipment.

STEP 13. Whether you have arranged for a site visit or have been encouraged to submit an application without a site visit, begin to fill in the application, responding specifically to what the funding agency is asking. Note: In some instances, the corporate or independent foundation does not provide an application. It merely will tell you to respond to its guidelines. If this is the case, it is recommended that you use a prototype application, making sure that you cover the needs, goals, objectives, activities, evaluation specifications, and budget. Some states have a common application form that is recognized by most foundations in the state. If this is the case, ask where you can obtain a copy of the application and study it carefully. Also, note that some corporations and foundations will ask for just a one or two-page letter of request. This you will appreciate very much. Always give the funding agency exactly what they ask for—nothing more, nothing less. After you have responded to the agency's guidelines and have completed a first draft of the application or letter, go over it carefully to correct spelling, typographical errors, grammar, and word usage.

STEP 14. Have one or two persons who are not in your field of interest read the completed application for clarity and input. Also, have one or two persons in your field of interest read it as well. Ask for assistance when formulating your budget, including proper budget categorizing and cost breakdowns. In many school districts, the person to go to for help is the business manager, district accountant, or site principal. It is essential to present to the funding agency a realistic, concise budget, providing explanations where appropriate.

STEP 15. After you have completed step 14, put together your final draft, including a cover letter that "grabs" the reader. The cover letter is usually one page and provides a brief summary of the project with all the necessary details. Obtain needed signatures and approvals, do the necessary proofreading, and make final corrections. Many funding agencies require that you file your application electronically. Others still require you to use the US Postal Service. Make certain that you are using the correct format for each agency to which you apply and give yourself enough time to meet the deadline.

Chapter 5

125 Foundations and Corporations Interested in Giving to K-12 Schools

The following foundations and corporations are interested in giving to K-12 schools. Their needs and goals may change from time to time, so make certain to do your homework before you contact them. Websites sometimes change as well, so double check to make sure that the web addresses are correct. There are some corporations and foundations interested in K-12 that have no website, especially family foundations. You can get more information about these foundations by contacting the foundation center website, http://www.foundationcenter.org. This list is not exhaustive by any means. There are many more foundations and corporations interested in giving to the schools. Search them out and add them to the list.

FUNDING AGENCY & WEB ADDRESSES

Andre Agassi Charitable Foundation
http://www.agassifoundation.org

J.A.& Katherine Albertson Foundation, Inc
http://www.jkaf.org

Paul G. Allen Virtual Education Foundation
http://www.pgafamilyfoundation.org

All State Foundation
http://www.allstatefoundation.org/

Herb Alpert Foundation
https://www.herbalpertfoundation.org/

The Annenberg Foundation
https://anneberg.org/

Laura & John Arnold Foundation
http://www.arnoldfoundation.org

Atlas Family Foundation
http://www.atlasfamilyfoundation.org

Arthur Vining Davis Foundation
https://www.avdf.org/

Bank of America Foundation
http://www.bankofamerica.com/foundation

Bezos Family Foundation
http://www.bezosfamilyfoundation.org/

Brady Education Foundation
http://www.bradyeducationfoundation.org/

NEC Foundation of America
http://www.necfoundation.org/

Oberkotter Foundation
https://oberkotterfoundation.org/

Best Buy Foundation
   http://www.bestbuy.com

Boeing Foundation
   http://www.boeing.com/

BJ's Charitable Foundation
   http://www.bjs.com

Charles Stewart Mott Foundation
   http://www.mott.org

Citi Foundation
   http://www.citifoundation.com

The Lynde & Harry Bradley Foundation, Inc.
   http://www.bradleyfdn.org

The Broad Foundation
   http://www.broadfoundation.org

Garth Brooks Foundation
   http://www.planetearth.com

The Brown Foundation, Inc.
   http://www.brownfoundation.org

J. Bulow Campbell Foundation
   http://www.jbcf.org

Barbara Bush Foundation
   http://www.barbarabushfoundation.com

Carnegie Foundation
   http://www.carnegiefoundation.org

The Annie E. Casey Foundation
   http://www.aecf.org

The Chicago Community Trust
ttp://www.cct.org

Cisco Systems Foundation
http://www.cisco.com/edu

The Edna McConnell Clark Foundation
http://www.emcf.org

Coca-Cola Foundation
http://www.coca-cola.com

The Corning Foundation
http://www.corning.com

Covenant Foundation, Inc.
http://www.covenantfn.org

Crail-Johnson Foundation
http://www.crail-johnson.org

Daniels Fund
http://www.danielsfund.org

Deere & Company
http://www.deere.com/

Dekko Foundation
http://www.dekkofoundation.org/

Michael and Susan Dell Foundation
http://www.msdf.org

Geraldine R. Dodge Foundation
http://www.grdodge.org

Donley Foundation
http://www.donleyfoundation.org/

The George Lucas Education Foundation
   http://www.edutopia.org

The Grammy Foundation
   http://www.grammyintheschools.com

Dow Chemical
   http://www.dow.com

Ewing Marion Kauffman Foundation
   http://www.kauffman.org

The Ford Foundation
   http://www.fordfound.org

Bill & Melinda Gates Foundation
   http://www.gatesfoundation.org

General Mills Foundation
   http://www.generalmills.com

Google Foundation
   http://www.google.org

Hasbro Children's Foundation
   http://www.hasbro.org

Golden Apple Foundation
   http://www.goldenapple.org

Hearst Foundation
   http://www.hearstfdn.org

Helios Education Foundation
   http://www.helios.org/

William & Flora Hewlett Foundation
   http://www.hewlett.org

The Home Depot Foundation
HTTP://corporate.homedepot.com/community

American Honda Foundation
http://www.hondacorporate.com

IBM Foundation
http://www.ibm.com

ING Foundation
http://www.ing.com

Intel Foundation
http://www.intel.com

International Business Machines
http://www.ibm.com

James Irvine Foundation
http://www.irvine.org

W.M. Keck Foundation
http://www.wmkeck.org

W.K. Kellogg Foundation
http://www.wkkf.org

John S. & James L. Knight Foundation
http://www.knightfoundation.org

Newman's Own
http://www.newmansown.com

Charles Lafitte Foundation
http://www.charleslafitte.org/

Lilly Endowment Inc.
http://www.lillyendowment.org

Lowes Charitable and Educational Foundation
http://www.toolboxforeducation.com

Lumina Foundation For Education
http://www.luminafoundation.org

John D. & Catherine T. MacArthur Foundation
http://www.mafound.org

Max and Marjorie Fisher Foundation
http://www.mmfisher.org/

The Malone Family Foundation
http://www.malonefamilyfoundation.com

McCall Kulak Family Foundation
http://www.mccallkulak.org/

Robert R. McCormick Foundation
http://www.mccormickfoundation.org/

McKnight Foundation
http://www.mcknight.org

The Meadows Foundation
http://www.mfi.org

Medtronic Foundation
http://www.medtronic.com/foundation

Metropolitan Life Insurance Co.
http://www.metlife.com

Meyer Memorial Trust
http://www.mmt.org

Microsoft Corporation
http://www.microsoft.com/giving

Milken Family Foundation
http://www.mff.org

The Mockingbird Foundation
http://www.mbird.org/

National Geographic Society
http://www.nationalgeographic.com

NEA Foundation
http://www.neafoundation.org

Newman's Own
http://www.newmansown.com

The New York Community Trust
http://www.nycommunitytrust.org

Open Society Foundations
http://www.opensocietyfoundations.org

Overdeck Family Foundation
http://www.overdeck.org/

Mr. Holland's Opus Foundation
http://www.mhopus.org

David & Lucille Packard Foundation
http://www.packard.org

The William Penn Foundation
http://www.williampennfoundation.org

J.C. Penney Company
http://www.jcpenney.net

PepsiCo Foundation
http://www.pepsico.com

Pew Charitable Trusts
http://www.pewtrusts.com

Peninsula Community Foundation
http://www.pcf.org

The Prudential Foundation
http://www.prudential.com/community/

Ralphs
http://www.ralphs.com

Robertson Foundation
http://www.robertsonfoundation.org

The Rockefeller Foundation
http://www.rockfound.org

The San Diego Foundation
http://www.sdfoundation.org

The San Francisco Foundation
http://www.sff.org

Charles & Lynn Schusterman Foundation
http://www.schusterman.org

Sea World Foundation
http://www.seaworld.org

Siemens Westinghouse Foundation
http://www.siemens-foundation.org

Silicon Valley Community Foundation
http://www.siliconvalleycf.org/

The Skillman Foundation
http://www.skillman.org

Alfred P. Sloan Foundation
http://www.sloan.org

The Sprint Foundation
http://www.sprint.com

George B. Storer Foundation
http://www.storerfoundation.org/

State Farm Foundation
http://www.statefarm.com

Stuart Foundation
http://www.stuartfoundation.org

Texas Instruments Foundation
http://www.ti.com

3M Foundation
https://www.3m.com

Toshiba America Foundation
http://www.taf.toshiba.com

Toyota Motor Sales
http://www.nsta.org/

Travelers Foundation
http://www.travelers.com

Verizon Foundation
http://www.verizon.com/foundation

The Wallace Foundation
http://www.wallacefunds.org

Walton Family Foundation
http://www.wffhome.com

Harry & Jeanette Weinberg Foundation
http://www.hjweinbergfoundation.org

Wells Fargo Foundation
http://www.wellsfargo.com

William T. Grant Foundation
http://www.wtgrantfoundation.org

Weyerhaeuser Company
http://www.weyerhaeuser.com

Robert W. Woodruff Foundation
http://www.woodruff.org

Tiger Woods Foundation
http://www.tgrfoundation.org

SC Johnson
http://www.scjohnson.com/

EARLY CHILDHOOD EDUCATION

There has been a great deal of interest in Early Childhood Education recently. These programs attempt to close the gap between children from low-income homes and children from more affluent homes. Because of the interest and because of the possibilities for additional funding in this area, I have added this new section to the book.

It is believed that the first five years of a child's life are when children build the social and emotional skills needed to succeed in school. On the first day of kindergarten, teachers expect children to be able to follow directions, start and finish projects, and know when they need to ask for help. These skills are as important as being able to count, recite

55

the alphabet, and write their names. If a child can't follow directions, he or she will have difficulty learning.

While many middle and upper-income children have early nurturing experiences, children in poverty often live in chaotic environments. Many low-income parents struggle to find a job or pay the bills and consequently don't have the means or time to create a stimulating home environment for their young children. It has been discovered that inequality in opportunity leads to an achievement gap that is evident as early as nine months of age and continues to inhibit students' progress throughout elementary school and beyond.

There is no proven strategy to close the achievement gap during the K-12 school years. But it has been discovered that high-quality early childhood education programs prevent the achievement gap from forming. Research on programs show that high-quality early childhood programs for children in need increase childhood literacy and high school graduation rates, as well as reducing crime and teenage pregnancy. Disadvantaged children who don't participate in high-quality early education programs are 50 percent more likely to be placed in special education classes and 25 percent are more likely to drop out of school. Additionally, 60 percent are more likely to never attend college, 70 percent more likely to be arrested for a violent crime, and 40 percent more likely to become a teen parent.

States around the country are grappling with the decision of whether or not to fund preschool as education dollars shrink. However, corporations and foundations have been showing increased interest. Following is a list of 26 Funders Interested in Giving to Early Childhood Education.

26 FUNDERS INTERESTED IN GIVING TO EARLY CHILDHOOD EDUCATION

Funding Agency Web Addresses

Paul M. Angell Foundation
http://pmangellfamfound.org/

Atlas Family Foundation
http://www.atlasfamilyfoundation.org/

Bezos Family Foundation
http://www.bezosfamilyfoundation.org/

Arthur M. Blank Family Foundation
https://blankfoundation.org/

Bohemian Foundation
http://www.bohemianfoundation.org/

Louis L. Borick Foundation
https://louislborickfoundation.org/

Brady Education Foundation
http://bradyeducationfoundation.org/

Buffet Early Childhood Fund
http://buffettearly.org/

Capital One Foundation
http://capitaloneinvestingforgood.com/

Annie E. Casey Foundation
http://www.aecf.org/

Child Welfare Foundation
http://www.cwf-inc.org/

Daniels Fund
   http://www.danielsfund.org/

Dekko Foundation
   http://www.dekkofoundation.org/

Frances R. Dewing Foundation
   http://www.frd-foundation.org/

Donley Foundation
   http://www.donleyfoundation.org

Einhorn Family Charitable Trust
   http://www.efct.org/

Max and Marjorie Fisher Foundation
   http://mmfisher.org/

Foundation for Child Development
   http://www.fcd-us.org/

Heising-Simons Foundation
   http://www.hsfoundation.org/

Helios Education Foundation
   http://www.helios.org/

W.K. Kellogg Foundation
   http://www.wkkf.org/

Robert R. McCormick Foundation
   http://donate.mccormickfoundation.org/

McCall Kulak Family Foundation
   http://www.mccallkulak.org/

J.B. and M.K. Pritzker Foundation
   http://pritzkerchildrensinitiative.org/

W. Clement & Jessie V. Stone Foundation
https://www.wcstonefnd.org/

Overdeck Family Foundation
https://overdeck.org/

SC Johnson
http://www.scjohnson.com/

George B. Storer Foundation
http://storerfoundation.org/

OTHER FOUNDATION RESOURCES

Foundation Directory Online
https://fconline.foundationcenter.org/

Community Foundations
http://www.foundations.org/
communityfoundations.html

Corporate and Private Foundations
http://www.foundations.org/grantmakers.html

Inside Philanthropy
http://www.insidephilanthropy.com/k-12-education/

Exponent Philanthropy
https://www.exponentphilanthropy.org/

Council on Foundations
http://www.cof.org/

GuideStar
http://www.guidestar.org/

http://www.guidestar.org/rxg/about-us/

Charity Navigator
http://www.charitynavigator.org/

Glass Pockets
http://glasspockets.org/

http://glasspockets.org/philanthropy-in-focus/
eye-on-the-giving-pledge/a-closer-look

Charter Schools
http://waltonfamilyfoundation.org/educationreform

http://gatesfoundation.org

Abbott Laboratories
http://www.abbott.com/responsibility/abbott-fund.html

JP Morgan Chase Foundation
http://www.jpmorganchase.com/corporate/
Corporate-Responsibility/global-philanthropy.htm

Corporate Money, 101
http://grantsandgiftsforschools.com/
CampusTechnology.pdf

Chevron Corporation
http://www.chevron.com/corporate-responsibility/
creating-prosperity/education/partners-programs

Cisco Systems Foundation
http://www.cisco.com/c/en/us/about/
csr/impact/cisco-foundation.html

Citigroup Foundation
https:// http://www.citigroup.com/citi/foundation/

Aerojet Rocketdyne
http://www.aerojetrocketdyne.com/foundation

Charles Hayden Foundation
   http://www.charleshaydenfoundation.org/

Hecksher Foundation for Children
   http://www.heckscherfoundation.org/

Hewlett-Packard Company
   https://www8.hp.com/us/en/hp-information/
   social-innovation/hp-foundation.html

Chapter 6

Cultivating and Connecting with Major Donors

Major donors can be defined by the scope and size of the organization to which they contribute. For example, major donors to Harvard or Stanford universities might be in the $1 million range, while major donors in your local school or district might be in the $5,000 range. You can set your own parameters for what you call major donors. For the purposes of this book, I will define a major donor as someone who contributes $10,000 or more to your cause.

Many prospective major donors are graduates of the public schools, live or work in our communities, own businesses or corporations in our communities, have children or grandchildren attending our schools, have taught or been administrators in our schools, are presently school board members or former school board members, or are volunteers interested in assisting the schools. A good number of these people are ready and able to make a major gift to your schools. Following are suggestions about how to connect with them.

MAKING THE CASE FOR SUPPORT

A case statement is essential when gearing up for a fundraising campaign. Whether you are working on annual giving, a capital campaign, planned giving, or corporate or foundation grants, it's important to work through questioning strategies written from a donor's prospective before you write the case statement. Here are some questions to consider:

1. Why are we contacting you at this time?

2. Why is there an urgent need for money?

3. Why is our solution unique?

4. What will happen if we don't get the money?

Tom Ahern, in his book *Seeing Through a Donor's Eyes*, recommends writing three case statements. The first statement is for internal use only and gathers as much information as possible about your organization and needs from a variety of key stakeholders. The second, a general case statement, should be short and sweet, summarizing what you are trying to do in about 100 words or less. The third case statement (the actual case statement) is made available to all who work on the campaign. Written from the donor's perspective, the case statement makes potential donors feel essential and important. Utilizing a four-step plan, the actual case statement will do the following:

1. Grabs your potential donor's attention.

2. Says something to your potential donor that builds interest.

3. Makes a promise to your potential donor that stimulates a desire to give.

4. Issues an urgent call to your potential
    donor to make a gift at this time.

A good case statement will vary in size and scope. I recommend four to six pages in length for K-12. Depending on your budget, it could be colorful and slick with photos and an attractive graphic design, or it could be straight forward and to the point. Jerold Panas in his new book, *Making a Case Your Donors Will Love* believes that the case statement "should be sufficiently inspiring and motivating to move the prospective donor from the mind to the heart to the checkbook." The case statements he has worked on are typically between 12 to 15 pages in length and in a three-ring binder because he believes that no one ever throws away a three-ring binder. He also marks the case statement with a rubber stamp that says "Draft" and asks potential major donors for input and suggestions for improvement.

A basic case statement should include all of the essential answers to the four-step plan above. Regardless of the nature of how the case statement is presented, it should inspire volunteers, board members, teachers, administrators, and others to donate first before they attempt to raise monies from others. The case statement instills confidence in all solicitors when they talk to people and when they go on visitations to ask for money. It serves as a ready-reference guide. I have found that people will give to your school or school district because the schools have personal meaning to them. Perhaps they went to your school, or their child or grandchild goes to the school at this time? Also, people will donate money to the schools because they believe in the public schools as a democratic institution in America. They want the schools to succeed.

For information and assistance on writing case statements,

including marketing and other forms of communications, see the links below.

WRITING YOUR CASE FOR SUPPORT

Seeing Through a Donor's Eyes, by Tom Ahern
http://emersonandchurch.com/bookstore/
seeing-through-a-donors-eyes/

Making a Case Your Donors Will Love, Jerold Panas
http://emersonandchurch.com/bookstore/
making-a-case-your-donors-will-love/

The Fundraiser's Guide to Irresistible Communications, by Jeff Brooks
http://emersonandchurch.com/bookstore/the-
fundraisers-guide-to-irresistible-communications/

The Money-Raising Nonprofit Brand, by Jeff Brooks
http://www.amazon.com/dp/1118583426/
ref=cm_sw_su_dp

12 WAYS TO CONNECT WITH MAJOR DONORS AFTER THE CASE FOR SUPPORT IS DEVELOPED

When approaching potential major donors, you are making a human connection that hopefully leads to a desired gift. Here are 12 ways to connect.

1. RECRUIT VOLUNTEERS in your community to work on the fundraising committee. Include prominent citizens; corporate and business executives; people with money; school administrators, including the superintendent; and principals, teachers, school board members, retired teachers, and others who have shown an interest in helping the schools.

2. DEVELOP A LIST OF PROSPECTS. The prospects become friends when the names become people. Work with the fundraising committee to identify the prospects and match up the volunteers who know the prospects as friends and relatives. Train the volunteers in using the case statement in their presentations.

3. IDENTIFY PEOPLE WITHIN YOUR FUNDRAISING COMMITTEE who have access to wealthy potential donors and make them part of your fundraising effort. It is easier for people to give to someone they know, rather than to strangers. Preserve friendships and try to separate solicitation from friendships. Those who are experienced givers know how to do this. In fact, they call upon each other for support of their favorite causes.

4. BRING IN AN OUTSIDE CONSULTANT OR A KNOWLEDGEABLE STAFF PERSON to conduct a comprehensive training program on how to connect with major donors in your community and elsewhere, how to use the case statement in your presentations, and how to use a database to compile and keep track of important fundraising information.

5. WHEN MAKING PERSONAL CONNECTIONS with prospective donors, let them do most of the talking. Show an interest in them. Good listening can give you many insights into their interests and needs. Learning how to turn acquaintances into beloved members of the school community is called "friendraising."

6. AFTER YOU RECEIVE A MAJOR GIFT, LEARN HOW TO SOLVE PROBLEMS for donors or help them with their interests. Show them that you care and make them part of your team. Ask for help or suggestions for improvement of your school, school district, or fundraising program.

7. MAINTAIN INTEGRITY IN THE OVERALL FUNDRAISING EFFORT. If you just go after the money without showing an interest in the prospective donor, the donor will sense that and may not give to your cause in the future.

8. REMEMBER TO SEND birthday cards, anniversary cards, get-well cards, congratulatory cards, thank-you notes, and the like to major donors. Thank-you notes via e-mail might be appropriate for some people, but not for others, especially older people.

9. PAY ATTENTION TO DONORS' CHILDREN. Praise them when appropriate. Parents love to hear good things about their kids from other people. Also, the kids of major donors will someday inherit the family's wealth from their parents and be looking for places to give. Why not your school or district?

10. LEARNING HOW TO BECOME GOOD STEWARDS of donors' monies is very important and reassuring. Donors want to know that their money is being invested wisely. If problems should arise, it's important that you keep donors informed about their gifts and deal honestly with them.

11. BEGIN THINKING ABOUT NAMING RIGHTS AS WELL AS MEMORIAL GIFTS. Colleges, universities, and private schools everywhere are doing this, so why not the public schools? If John Smith wants to give you $3 million for the creative and performing arts center, why not suggest naming the building the John Smith Creative and Performing Arts Center?

12. DO NOT IGNORE SMALL DONORS. Learn how to turn the casual small donor into a major donor. The small donor of yesterday can become the big donor of tomorrow, especially if the donor suddenly inherits a lot of money or properties.

If your district's needs are like so many others across the country, learning how to connect with major donors is critical if you want your share of the fundraising pie. Connecting with these donors in human terms and making them friends of the schools is one of the major tasks of public school fundraisers in the 21st century.

FINDING WEALTHY DONORS

Colleges, universities, private schools, nonprofits, and churches are very adept at finding wealthy donors within their communities and among their alumni and friends. They also know that there are consultant companies that specialize in this area and are available to assist them. It has been my experience that regardless of where you are located in the United States, whether it is in a rural area, big city, or the suburbs, there are wealthy people living there. You have to dig hard! Many times they might be your next-door neighbor. Take a look at the book The Millionaire Next Door, by Thomas Stanley and William Danko http://www.thomasjstanley.com/publication/the-millionaire-next-door/.

People with money in your community who have attended your schools, have relatives attending your schools, have taught or been administrators in your schools, or are involved in your schools at this time are most likely to give to your cause. All these people are potential donors. Nurture these people with gusto! Treat them with dignity and respect and become their friends. You won't believe the payoff!

Asking for money from friends, relatives, or strangers is an unnatural act. Most of us don't know how to or don't want to do this. But it's not all that difficult once you learn how. When approaching a potential donor, you are making a human connection over time that hopefully will lead to a desired gift. My more than 40 years of experience has helped me to understand that individuals don't want to give their money away, but they do want to invest in worthy causes that change people's lives. There are few causes more worthy and more life-altering than public education.

INHERITED WEALTH

When it comes to studying and understanding wealth in America over the years, I have relied on the research and writings of Paul Schervish and John Havens, who were researchers at the Center on Wealth and Philanthropy at Boston College in Chestnut Hill, Massachusetts. In a number of their studies they projected that people throughout the United States will be inheriting a total of $41 trillion by the year 2052, a number that is based on a 2 percent growth rate. They further indicated that with a growth rate of 3 percent, $73 trillion will be inherited, and with a growth rate of 4 percent, that number will increase to $132 trillion. They also reported that the baby boomer generation (ages 50 to 68) will keep fundraisers busy for many years to come because they are wealthier in total and per household than any previous generation and are just now coming into prime giving ages. In addition to the boomer generation, Schervish and Havens recommended in their studies that we continue to solicit from prospective donors older than 68 as well as those under age 50 who are just coming into inherited wealth. If Schervish and Havens are correct in their projections, public schools all over the nation that are ready and able to solicit major donors will reap major rewards.

Below you will find links to websites that will be of help to you. Some of the links lead to classic books written by some of the biggest names in fundraising in America. Also included are links to discovering wealth in America and how to approach the people who have it. Of particular interest is the Center on Wealth and Philanthropy at Boston College, where some of the foremost research has taken place, and the Giving USA Reports, where you can get a yearly update on fundraising in the United States and get a feel for what's happening across the nation and a breakdown of where grants come from and who gets them.

FUNDRAISING, MARKETING, & COMMUNICATIONS

The Essential Fundraising Guide for K-12 Schools, 1st Edition, by Stan Levenson
   http://www.stanlevenson.com

Asking, by Jerold Panas
   http://emersonandchurch.com/bookstore/asking/

Mega Gifts, by Jerold Panas
   http://emersonandchurch.com/bookstore/mega-gifts/

How to Connect with Donors, by Thomas Wolf
http://emersonandchurch.com/bookstore/how-to-connect-with-donors-and-double-the-money-you-raise/

Rural Schools Fundraising, by Stan Levenson
https://blog.getedfunding.com/rural-fundraising/

How to Turn Your Words Into Money, by Jeff Brooks
http://www.amazon.com/Turn-Your-Words-Into-Money/dp/1889102555/ref=sr_1_1?crid=24XG5HVKJ3Y6Z

The Givers, by David Callahan
http://www.amazon.com/Givers-Wealth-Power-Philanthropy-Gilded/dp/1101947055/ref=sr_1_1?keywords=The+Givers&qid=1556311910&s=books&sr=1-1

LOCATING WEALTHY DONORS

America's Top Donors
http://philanthropy.com/factfile/gifts

http://www.philanthropynewsdigest.org/news/charitable-giving-grew-13-percent-in-2013-atlas-of-giving-estimates

http://www.jgacounsel.com/resources

Center on Wealth and Philanthropy, Boston College
http://www.bc.edu/research/cwp/

Giving USA Reports
https://givingusa.org/

DonorPerfect
http://www.donorperfect.com/

Wealth Engine
  http://www.WealthEngine.com

Equilar
  http://www.equilar.com/fundraising.html

News Bank
  https://www.newsbank.com/

Google Alerts
  http://www.google.com/alerts

Blackbaud
  https://www.blackbaud.com/

Reeher
  http://www.reeher.com/resources/

Ellucian
  http://www.ellucian.com/fundraising-software/

National Center for Charitable Statistics
  https://nccs.urban.org/

Resources for Nonprofits
  http://www.idealist.org/info/Nonprofits

Philanthropy Roundtable
  http://www.philanthropyroundtable.org

Women's Philanthropy Institute
  https://philanthropy.iupui.edu/institutes/
  womens-philanthropy-institute/index.html

National Philanthropic Trust
  http://www.nptrust.org/

Chapter 7

Annual Campaigns, Capital Campaigns, and Planned Giving

ANNUAL CAMPAIGNS

Annual campaigns are ongoing yearly appeals that provide general operating support for the schools. Gifts tend to be smaller than capital campaign gifts, which have loftier goals. New donors are solicited each year in an annual campaign and previous donors are asked to increase their contributions from the prior year. Because monies are usually given out of the income of the donor, spouses do not have to be consulted when approaching donors in an annual campaign. School or district foundation members, staff, parents, administrators, or volunteers can solicit these gifts, and while personal visits or gatherings are desirable, they are not mandatory. Gifts of cash are the most prevalent type given in an annual campaign.

Some of the fundraising approaches used in annual campaigns are Internet fundraising, direct mail solicitation, donor newsletters, phonathons, radio and TV solicitation, and special events.

CAPITAL CAMPAIGNS

Capital campaigns have bigger goals than annual campaigns and because of this, gift requests for the schools are set far higher. Capital campaigns are very new to the public schools, and some school districts are beginning to recognize this tremendous potential resource for external fundraising. Time frames in capital campaigns are generally extended, such as a three-year (or a five-year) campaign to build new facilities such as a new creative and performing arts center. Prospects are asked to give or pledge a certain amount of money over time. Capital campaigns are an exciting period in a school community because the goals are tangible and the results are highly visible. These campaigns are usually organized for endowment purposes, as well as for buildings and equipment. People who make a major gift to a capital campaign receive great joy over their lifetime.

LEAD GIFTS AND NAMING RIGHTS

I have found that identifying one or more people in the community or a corporate sponsor to make a "lead gift" before the capital campaign officially begins is a good way to get started. One way to obtain a lead gift is to provide the opportunity for the donor to have a facility on campus named in his or her family's honor; for example, "The Guzman Family Performing Arts Center." This is done all the time in the private schools, colleges, and universities, and we are beginning to see it happen in the public schools.

Once the lead gift is made, funding opportunities for naming other portions of the facility should be made available. Using the example above, donors could also receive public recognition for funding the main lobby, the stage, the lighting, the dressing rooms, the seats, and others. The opportunity for recognition and service is why capital campaigns have such great appeal to prospective donors and why many donors become motivated to make major contributions.

Named gifts have been around for a long time on private school campuses, at colleges and universities, and at nonprofit facilities like YMCAs, YWCAs, and Boys and Girls Clubs. A number of public school districts are taking a close look at this fundraising opportunity and realizing that the schools are a wonderful place for a family to leave a lasting legacy by having a school building, a cafeteria, a ball field, or a seat in a little theater named after them. In addition, schools and school districts are exploring ways of giving commercial vendors and corporations opportunities for Naming Rights, especially as they relate to gymnasiums, ball fields, auditoriums, stadiums, signage, and track-and-field facilities. If you move in this direction, it is recommended that the Naming Rights be awarded for a specific period of time (five to ten years, more or less), after which new negotiations take place or the contract is rescinded.

Since this book was first published, a lot has been going on related to Naming Rights in the public schools. In Texas where high school football is such a big thing, a number of school districts have negotiated Naming Rights for athletic fields, buildings, and performing arts groups. Other Texas school districts have negotiated Naming Rights for telecommunications and broadcasting as well as refreshment venues. It is important to point out that the Internal Revenue Service has become particularly concerned about Naming Rights of sports facilities because of the perception that such facilities provide unique commercial value. Note: Check with Federal tax counsel for tax implications of Naming Rights for performing arts centers, soccer fields, football stadiums, and basketball arenas before consummation of such agreements take place to determine whether such agreements may be interpreted by the IRS as private business use.

Below is a sampling of schools and school districts that already have negotiated naming rights with their donors totaling in the millions of dollars:

UPDATED SAMPLING OF SCHOOLS AND SCHOOL DISTRICTS THAT HAVE NEGOTIATED NAMING RIGHTS

1. At Brunswick High School in Northeastern Ohio, a regional automotive complex purchased the rights of the football complex as part of a 10 year agreement for $750,000.

2. In Circleville, Ohio, Berger Health Care paid $190,000 for the Naming Rights of the field house and Coughlin Automotive paid $40,000 for the new scoreboard at the football stadium.

3. Westfield Washington Schools in Indiana agreed on a 10-year, $1.2 million Naming Rights deal to help build a 5,000-seat football stadium.

4. In Riverside, Illinois Schools a member of the community Jerry Kennelly bought the naming rights in a 20-year, $140,000 donation to name the athletic complex after his great-uncle Martin Kennelly.

5. Worcester High Schools, in Worcester, Massachusetts, now play football at Commerce Bank Field at Foley Stadium.

6. Antioch High School, Nashville, Tennessee now has an Academy of Business and Finance

7. McGavock High School, Nashville, Tennessee now has an Academy of Digital Design and Communication

8. Cony High School, in Augusta, Maine, has sponsors for travel bags for their basketball team, scoreboard sponsorship, and gym floor logos.

9. Central High School, in Little Rock, Arkansas, plays at Quigley-Cox Stadium at Verizon Wireless Field.

10. Springboro High School, in Springboro, Ohio, plays football at CareFlight Field.

11. Toms River Regional Schools, New Jersey, plays at Poland Springs Arena, sponsored by Nestle Waters North America, Incorporarted.

12. Gloucester High School, in Gloucester, Massachusetts, has a New Balance Track and Field at Newell Stadium.

13. Sun Prairie High School in Sun Prairie, Wisconsin now has a Summit Credit Union Baseball Field.

14. Presque Isle Middle School Sports Complex, in Presque Isle, Maine, sold logos to sponsors.

15. Escondido H.S., Escondido, CA plays football at the Wilson Stadium at Chick Embrey Field

NUMBER AND SIZE OF GIFTS NEEDED TO ACHIEVE A CAMPAIGN GOAL

Over the years, fundraising professionals at the college, university, and private schools have been following industry standards related to the number and size of gifts needed to achieve a campaign goal. Your school or school district might want to take a serious look at this as a possible guide based upon your community's giving ability. For example, with a $50,000 or $1 million campaign goal, the number and size of gifts needed to achieve your desired outcome, might look like the examples below:

$50,000 GOAL

2 gifts @ $20,000 each for a total of	$40,000
5 gifts @ $1,000 each for a total of	$5,000
10 gifts @$500 each for a total of	$5,000
Total	**$50,000**

$1 MILLION GOAL

1 gift of $500,000 for a total of	$500,000
2 gifts of $150,000 for a total of	$300,000
5 gifts of $10,000 for a total of	$50,000
20 gifts of $1,000 for a total of	$20,000
50 gifts of $100 for a total of	$5,000
1,000 gifts of $25 for a total of	$125,000
Total	**$1,000,000**

NOTE: The above is an example only. Note the pyramid effect. A small number of donors, if approached effectively, can carry the major burden of a capital campaign. You can have other goals and work out similar charts. Your school, school district, or foundation should do the projections based upon your donor pool, size, ability to give, and needs.

PLANNED GIVING

Planned giving refers to the process of making a charitable gift of cash or non-cash assets to one or more nonprofit organizations, including the public schools. Charitable gifts are a tangible way for donors to contribute to the schools. The gift, when made, usually requires consideration and planning in light of the donor's overall estate plan and tax situation. Legal documents to be completed should be made part of the donor's overall estate plan and should be coordinated in cooperation with the donor's financial advisors.

There are many tax advantages for giving cash and non-cash assets to the schools, including appreciated assets. While gifts of cash are always welcome, stock, bonds, shares in mutual funds, a home or farm property, vacant land, vacation or rental property, commercial or income property, life insurance, and other non-cash gifts can be made to the schools. Because of the size and potential impact of such gifts on an estate, a donor should be advised to consult with his or her professional advisors before completing the process. Additionally, the school district should consult with its legal advisors concerning implementation of a planned giving program and develop policies to receive and administer such gifts, as well as policies for rejecting certain gifts.

As part of an overall estate plan, a donor may choose to make a gift to the schools over time—that is, a gift made after the donor no longer needs the asset. The gifts may earn a donor a charitable tax deduction at the time of the gift, while increasing the donor's income level during his or her lifetime and lowering the donor's estate taxes.

There are also tax advantages when giving cash and non-cash assets to a nonprofit organization such as a school or a local education foundation. Giving non-cash assets may be attractive to supporters of the schools in that they are donating to a good cause, and there are favorable tax implications for this kind of gift. Examples of appreciated assets are:

1. Stocks

2. Bonds

3. Shares in mutual funds

4. A home or farm property

5. Vacant land

6. Vacation or rental property

7. Commercial property

8. Other assets held in a form other than in cash

Property that has increased in value and has been owned on a long-term basis generally brings the most in tax savings for the donor. People also find that giving non-cash property leaves their cash available for other purposes. Most long-term appreciated property is deductible for its full fair market value when the gift is made to a school or district foundation. In addition, capital gains tax is not due on property that is donated rather than sold. Under current law, gifts of appreciated property worth up to 30 percent of the donor's adjusted gross income can be deducted in the year of the gift and excess deductions may be carried over into as many as the next five years if deductions are itemized. There are many ways to make gifts of appreciated and marketable securities and real property to the schools that provide significant tax advantages for the donor. In either case, a tax attorney or other certified accountant should be consulted before any transfer of ownership is made.

The next section discusses cash and non-cash gifts and presents an explanation of gifts that could be given to schools outright or bequeathed upon the death of the donor.

OUTRIGHT GIFT OF CASH

An outright gift of cash for some people is the most comfortable gift to give. It would also be very much appreciated by the schools, in that cash is easy to administer and can be used for multiple purposes. Many philanthropists give cash gifts to worthy causes and are more comfortable giving in this manner. Sometimes people have a specific cause to which they want to contribute and will so designate. This is referred to as a restrictive gift. Others will give cash and not place any restrictions on how the money is spent. This is considered an unrestrictive gift. Needless to say, unrestrictive gifts offer more flexibility than restrictive gifts. However, any gifts of cash are always appreciated.

APPRECIATED MARKETABLE SECURITIES

One of the most attractive methods for givers to realize their charitable intentions toward the schools is in giving appreciated marketable securities. A gift of listed stocks, bonds, or other publicly traded securities entitles the giver to a charitable income tax deduction equal to the full fair market value of the securities on the date of the gift, provided that the securities were owned for at least one year. In addition, the donor does not incur capital gains tax on the transfer of such securities to the schools.

ENTIRE INTEREST IN REAL ESTATE

An outright gift of unencumbered real estate may enable the giver to make a significant gift to the schools without incurring capital gains tax on the transfer of the appreciated asset. The gift will entitle the giver to a charitable income tax deduction equal to the fair market value of the interest in the property on the date of the transfer, provided that the property was owned for more than one year.

CHARITABLE REMAINDER TRUST

A charitable remainder trust is a unique gift opportunity available to people who own a primary residence, a second home, or a farm and wish to dispose of such property in their estate to the schools but want to continue using the property for their lifetime. They may give the schools a remainder interest in their property, retain the property for the rest of their lives, and receive income for the rest of their lives.

TANGIBLE PERSONAL PROPERTY

A person might wish to consider making a gift of personal property such as art objects, books, and other collectibles to the schools. If the schools can use the gift of such property toward the furtherance of the educational mission and the property has been owned for more than one year, the giver will be eligible for a fair market value charitable income tax deduction without having to recognize the capital gain on any appreciation and will receive a tax credit for the fair market value of the property.

LIFE INSURANCE

If a person owns a life insurance policy and no longer requires its protection, he or she may wish to consider transferring ownership of the policy to the schools, or to name the schools as a beneficiary to receive all or a portion of the policy proceeds. Another possibility is to purchase a new policy and transfer ownership to the schools. Each gift will generate a charitable income tax deduction roughly equal to the cash surrender value of the policy on the date of the gift. A person might also want to use the cash value of policies that have "outlived" their original purposes to immediately give a gift to the schools.

SOCIAL SECURITY CHECKS

There are many people all across America whose retirement lifestyle does not require the income they receive from social security. Donating these benefits to the public schools would not only give donors great satisfaction, but would also reduce their overall tax bill. Potential donors can sign paperwork authorizing their bank to automatically send part or all of the proceeds of their social security check to your school or school district. Make certain that potential donors consult with their tax advisors before going ahead with this plan.

BEQUESTS

A bequest is a gift from a person's will or living trust to the schools after they are no longer with us. This is a very popular way to make a deferred gift. Here are eight generally accepted approaches for donors making a bequest to the schools.

1. SPECIFIC BEQUEST. This is a gift of a specific item to a specific beneficiary. For example, "I give my 2012 Mercedes-Benz to XYZ School." If that specific property has been disposed of before death, the bequest fails and no claim can be made to any other property. (In other words, XYZ School cannot claim some other property.)

2. GENERAL BEQUEST. This is usually a gift of a stated sum of money. It will not fail, even if there is not sufficient cash to meet the bequest. For example, "I give $50,000 to XYZ High School." If there is only $2,500 cash in the estate, other assets must be sold to meet the bequest.

3. CONTINGENT BEQUEST. This is a bequest made on condition that a certain event must occur before distribution to the beneficiary. For example, "I give $100,000 to XYZ School provided that Mr. Jones remains the principal for the next five years." A contingent bequest is specific in nature and fails if the condition is not met.

4. RESIDUARY BEQUEST. This is a gift of all the "rest, residue, and remainder" of the donor's estate after all other bequests, debts, and taxes have been paid. A school or school district can be named in a person's estate to receive a residuary bequest.

5. UNRESTRICTED BEQUEST. This is a gift made to a school or school district that can be used for general purposes, at the discretion of the school board. A gift like this—without conditions attached—is frequently the most useful, as it allows the school or school district to determine the wisest and most pressing need for the funds at the time of receipt.

6. RESTRICTED BEQUEST. This type of gift allows the donor to specify how the funds are to be used. For example, "The gift is to be used to build a new creative and performing arts center for XYZ High School." Potential givers of restricted gifts to individual schools and school districts should be encouraged to discuss their plans and ideas with the building principal, the superintendent of schools, and anyone else who needs to know.

7. HONORARY OR MEMORIAL BEQUEST. This gift is given "in honor of" or "in memory of" someone. For example, "The gift in the amount of $1,000,000 is given in honor of my dear mother, Mabel Montgomery to the XYZ School District."

8. ENDOWED BEQUEST. This bequest allows donors to restrict the principal of their gift, requiring the school district to hold the funds permanently and use only the investment income they generate. Creating an endowment in this manner means that your gift can continue on in perpetuity.

CHARITABLE GIFT ANNUITIES

A donor can provide a gift to the school or school district while receiving income for the remainder of his/her life and the life of a loved one. This kind of a gift can increase a person's income while providing tax benefits immediately for the donor's estate. It also allows the donor to make more significant gifts to the schools than would otherwise be possible. An example of this would be a husband and wife who own their house free and clear. Through a charitable gift of the home to a school or school district, the couple could live in the home for the remainder of their lives, while receiving income and tax benefits for the remainder of their lives.

*Notes: All information pertaining to tax benefits listed above is subject to change. Federal and state tax laws change on a continuing basis. In working with potential donors, encourage them to talk with their accountants and/or tax attorneys concerning any of the above. Accompany them, if they so desire, to discuss their objectives and the opportunities available to them. Involve the attorneys for the school district as well. For additional information on planned giving, see publications in the bibliography.

Following are links to additional information on annual campaigns, capital campaigns, and planned giving to broaden your prospective and make you aware of how important this phase of fundraising is.

ANNUAL CAMPAIGNS

http://www.ipsf.net/about-us.html

https://blog.cdsfunds.com/the_capital_campaign_plan_road_map_to_success

http://www.ncsota.org/agc/

http://www.headsupsr.org/

Capital Campaign Announcements, Materials, and Forms

http://www.herronhighschool.org/news/

http://www.kinkaid.org/giving

http://urbanadamah.org/about-us/capital-campaign/

Planned Giving, Estate Planning, and Gifts

The Big Gift, by Stan Levenson
http://www.grantsandgiftsforschools.com/TheBigGift.htm

Planned Giving Design Center
http://www.pgdc.com/

Planned Giving Dot Com
http://www.plannedgiving.com/

Sample Bequest Language
http://kpbs.giftlegacy.com/?pageID=127

Gifts of Stock

http://www.cresmanager.com/
AutoPDF/gleg_ebroch_download.
pdf?CID=1051&id=158&PID=DP-2013-55.1-pw

Gifts of Real Estate

http://www.pgdc.com/pgdc/gifts-real-estate

Gifts of Art

http://www.pgdc.com/pgdc/expert-advice-
donations-art-charitable-organizations

http://wealthmanagement.com/blog/
charitable-gifts-artworks-part-1

Chapter 8

Communication and Social Media
Online Giving

The Chronicle of Philanthropy reported in 2013 that online gifts to America's nonprofits rose more than 14 percent over the previous year to $2.1 billion. They also reported that online giving is growing far faster than all other types of donations. It seems clear that many donors want to give from their desktops, smartphones, and tablets. They find this approach to be comfortable, and it saves them time and energy.

Many nonprofits are reporting an overall increase in online giving by encouraging donors to make online gifts monthly, quarterly, semiannually, or at another set period of time. Of all the online giving approaches, many development officers agree that monthly giving is one of the most reliable forms, through which donors are least likely to discontinue their support. From an administrative perspective, online giving is efficient and simple to operate.

It was reported in the Chronicle of Philanthropy back in 2014 that a number of colleges, universities, and nonprofits received online gifts of $100,000 or more and the University of Texas M.D. Anderson Cancer Center received an online gift of $1 million. At that time, the Chronicle of Philanthropy projected that $1 out of $5 could soon be donated electronically. My observations tell me at this time that at least $2 out of $5 is being donated electronically to the public schools. What are the implications for being so bullish about online giving, and why should this matter to schools and school districts? It matters because all trends point in the direction of online giving as a viable and timesaving way of donating to the schools. This is the way that many people like to give, and the trend should continue into the future.

At the present time, many public school foundations are actively seeking online donations. There is no research data available to show how successful they have been. It is my best estimate based upon my contacts in the field that online giving in the public schools has increased at least 14 percent over the previous year, just as it has for America's nonprofits.

There are more than 2 billion people connected to the Internet worldwide. The potential for raising serious online dollars is enormous. If your school, district, foundation, P.T.A. or P.T.O. is not involved in raising monies online, it's time to begin. See below for more assistance.

In addition to raising money online, there are other ways to raise money including direct mail solicitation, donor newsletters, mobile (telephone), radio, television, and special events. Let's take a look at all these.

DIRECT MAIL SOLICITATION

Direct mail is a very practical way to reach many small gift prospects within your school community without having to recruit and train a big workforce. Once a good letter is drafted, a small group of volunteers can handle this type of solicitation.

An effective fundraising letter makes an appeal from one person (or family) to another. It gives recipients an opportunity to support a worthy cause while meeting their personal needs of wanting to help the schools. It also invites them to make a specific gift that will have a positive impact on the schools and explains the benefits derived from making the gift. Mal Warwick, in his book *How to Write Successful Fundraising Appeals*, talks about six qualities that are shared by the most productive fundraising appeals. These are clarity, cohesiveness, authenticity, ease of response, appropriateness, and engaging copy. For more information, go to: http://www. amazon.com/How-Write-Successful-Fundraising-Appeals/dp/1118543661

DONOR NEWSLETTERS

More and more authorities in the field, including Tom Ahern and Jeff Brooks, believe that a well-thought-out letter to constituents, especially older ones, will reap major financial rewards in our annual campaigns. Good newsletters might spark some interest in giving to your major campaign as well. Ahern talks about newsletters enhancing donor retention by reporting on the impact donors' gifts have on the world. He also points out that good newsletters express love for and bring joy and elements of surprise to the donor. According to Ahern, the style of writing in a newsletter is very important. He cautions that corporate communications are not what donors are looking for. I would add that school jargon is not what donors are looking for. Rather, typical donors are seeking an emotional connection. They make decisions on their emotions. If something feels good to them, they give. If they feel loved and appreciated, they give some more. Brooks, a communications specialist, points out that the donor-focused newsletter should remind the donor what an incredible difference he or she makes. He believes that most donors won't give unless they have a good reason to give now. And when donors receive urgent fundraising messages, they know they have a role in making the world a better place. They get excited about how much their gift matters, and they want to respond accordingly.

TELEPHONE, MOBILE PHONES, RADIO, AND TELEVISION

Using these media can be worthwhile if proper preparation and training take place and the community is informed of your intentions, including dates and times to expect your call, or dates and times that you will be conducting your telethon or radio solicitation.

Telephone solicitation has been around for years. We have all heard from the colleges and universities we attended, haven't we? This kind of solicitation takes a lot of training and practice with scripts prepared ahead of time. Overcoming objections is important to learn, as well as how to respond to being put off. There are a number of consultants and consultant companies that specialize in this type of solicitation, including companies that will do this for you for a price. See below.

Mobile phone giving is relatively new. It brings the power and reach of mobile phones to schools and school districts. It is an effective means for new donor acquisition, fundraising, and donor interaction.

Some local radio and TV stations, as a public service, are donating airtime to schools and school districts around the country. In some instances, TV and radio personalities are assisting in the fundraising effort. Ask for some of this airtime to fundraise and request some volunteer assistance. There's money out there if you put in the time and effort.

SPECIAL EVENTS

A number of schools and school districts around the country are raising serious dollars sponsoring special events like golf tournaments, tennis tournaments, 5K and 10K runs and walks, dinner-dances, and silent auctions. In San Diego County, where I live, schools such as Coronado High School and Torrey Pines High School raise between $100,000 and $200,000 in one evening at their annual dinner-dances that include a silent auction. Of course, it should be mentioned that these schools are located in some of our most affluent areas! The following should be considered when planning special events for K-12:

1. What are your goals for conducting the special event?

2. How much money are your trying to raise?

3. Do you have any sponsors or underwriters for the event?

4. Do you have adequate staffing to run the event?

5. Is the event appropriate for your group's purpose and mission?

6. Is your board aware of the event and do they know what is expected of them?

7. Are you reasonably certain that the event will net you enough money in relationship to the amount of time, effort, and money invested?

SOME MOBILE APPS TO SIMPLIFY FUNDRAISING

In most school districts fundraisers are busy people. They wear many hats. Sometimes one person is handling everything including grant writing, corporate, foundation, and government grants, and grants and gifts from individual donors. In other school districts there is a cadre of people specializing in each fundraising area. Mobile apps for fundraising are here but are not used extensively in K-12 schools. However, we are beginning to see mobile apps being used in fundraising at the colleges, universities, and non-profits. As mentioned elsewhere, we have much to learn from these entities.

Below you will find a host of links that cover most facets of donor communication and social media including mobile fundraising apps and how they are being used today. Also included are examples of some of the leading K-12 foundation websites from around the country. The websites will give you some insight as to how they are set up to do online fundraising and how each communicates with its constituents.

DONOR COMMUNICATIONS AND SOCIAL MEDIA

The Fundraisers Guide to Irresistible Communications, by Jeff Brooks
http://www.emersonandchurch.com/products/the-fundraisers-guide-to-irresistible-communications/

How to Turn Your Words Into Money, by Jeff Brooks
http://www.emersonandchurch.com/products/how-to-turn-your-words-into-money/

Making Money With Donor Newsletters, by Tom Ahern
http://www.emersonandchurch.com/products/making-money-with-donor-newsletters/

Nonprofit Website Elements
https://npengage.com/nonprofit-marketing/10-
must-have-elements-for-nonprofit-websites/

Grant Funding with Social Media
http://www.edutopia.org/blog/grant-
funding-with-social-media-brian-dixon

Mobile Giving
http://www.mobilegiving.org/

http://www.mobilecause.com/

Razoo
https://www.mightycause.com/

Crowdfunding
http://www.crowdfunding.com/

Kickstarter
http://www.kickstarter.com/hello?ref=homepage

Schoola
http://www.schoola.com

Fundraising and Tech Resources for Tech Integration
http://www.edutopia.org/blog/grants-fundraising-
tech-integration-mary-beth-hertz

MOBILE APPS FOR FUNDRAISING

6 Apps to Simplify Fundraising Tasks, Chronicle of Philanthropy
http://philanthropy.com/article/6-Apps-
to-Simplify-Fundraising/145199/

5 Mobile Fundraising Apps for Do-Gooders and Nonprofits, Nonprofit Tech For Good
> http://www.nptechforgood.com/2013/10/31/5-mobile-fundraising-apps-for-do-gooders-and-nonprofits/

Artez Interactive
> http://www.frontstream.com/artez/

A SAMPLING OF 25 FOUNDATION WEBSITES FOR K-12

Below is a sampling of 25 foundation websites for K-12. Included are two websites for charter schools. Study these websites. Compare them with your school or district website. How does each foundation raise monies online? What does each website feature? How easy is it to access and donate monies to each site? What can you learn from some of these websites to improve your site and raise more monies? (*Charter Schools)

The Fund for Public Schools, NYC
> https://www.fundforpublicschools.org/

Houston Independent School District Foundation, TX
> http://www.houstonisdfoundation.org

The Foundation for the Oklahoma City Schools, OK
> http://okckids.com/

Public School 6, NYC
> http://www.ps6nyc.org/

*Da Vinci Schools, CA
> http://davincischools.org

High Tech High, CA
  http://www.hightechhigh.org/

Ogden School Foundation, UT
  http://ogdenschoolfoundation.org

Irvine Public Schools Foundation, CA
  http://www.ipsf.net/

Alexandria School District 206 Education Foundation, MN
  http://www.alexandria.k12.mn.us/page/82

Bellevue Schools Foundation, WA
  http://www.bellevueschoolsfoundation.org

Northshore Schools Foundation, WA
  http://www.northshoreschoolsfoundation.org/

Eureka Schools Foundation, CA
  http://www.eurekaschoolsfoundation.org/

Laguna Beach Education Foundation, CA
  http://www.lbschoolpower.org/

The Foundation for Lee County Public Schools, FL
  http://www.leeschoolfoundation.org/

Miami-Dade County Schools, FL
  http://www.giveourstudentstheworld.org/

Chicago Public Schools, IL
  http://thefundchicago.org/invest-
  in-chicagos-public-schools/

The Foundation for Madison's Public Schools, WI
  http://www.fmps.org/

The Portland Public Schools Foundation, OR
http://allhandsraised.org/what-we-do/
our-impact/ppsfoundation/

The Mill Valley Schools Community Foundation, CA
http://kiddo.org/about-kiddo/

Lawrence Township Education Foundation, NJ
http://www.ltefnj.org/

The Westport Education Foundation, MA
http://www.westporteducationfoundation.com/

Norwalk Education Foundation, CT
http://www.norwalkeducation.org/

Philadelphia Education Fund. PA
http://www.philaedfund.org/

Chapel Hill-Carrboro Public School Foundation, NC
http://www.publicschoolfoundation.org/

Virginia Beach Education Foundation, VA
http://www.vbef.org/

Chapter 9

Administering the Fundraising Program

WHY YOU NEED A DEVELOPMENT OFFICE

Tax-supported state colleges and universities have faced similar budget constraints as the public schools over the years, yet have figured out ways to deliver world-class learning programs by establishing big-time development offices and raising millions of dollars year in and year out. These institutions of higher education know how to do this and we have much to learn from them. We are fast learners and things are beginning to happen!

Some school districts, including public charter schools are discovering what the universities and colleges have already learned, that development offices, staffed by experienced, competent people, are the way to go. As such, we are seeing these offices beginning to crop up in school districts across the country. The size of these offices are minuscule compared to the public colleges and universities; however, it's important to note that they are there, and they are getting larger as school boards understand their value. At this time some school districts have only volunteers working in development; some have one or two-person development offices working with volunteers; others, like big city school districts, have a staff of people working in development.

A number of school districts have development offices as part of their 501c3 foundations. These offices vary in size and capability based upon the staff's expertise and the financial resources of the community. Regardless of the size and make-up of development offices found in the schools today, it's a very positive sign that they are there and we are beginning to understand their value. School districts have discovered that once a development office is established and staffed by experienced, competent people, it takes about two years or less to become a profit center. What a deal!

STAFFING THE DEVELOPMENT OFFICE

Depending on the district's size, the development office might consist of one or more staff members wearing many hats. In a large-scale fundraising effort, the staff might be organized in the following way:

Director of Development
Has overall responsibility for the district's total fundraising effort. This includes supervising the development office staff and serving as the liaison with school sites and school and district foundations. The Director will have extensive fundraising experience at the school or district level.

Director of Alumni Relations
Everyone who has attended public schools in the USA has been influenced by one or more favorite teachers at the preschool, elementary school, middle school, junior high, or high school levels. Because of this, it's important to identify alumni from all these levels. The Director of Alumni

Relations works cooperatively with Principals and their staff to identify as many alumni as they can. The Director also meets with alumni groups at each school, further identifies other alumni, and solicits their input for improving the school(s). The Director of Alumni Relations in cooperation with fundraising staff and principals solicits grants and gifts from alumni including annual gifts, capital gifts, lead gifts, planned giving, and naming rights among others.

Director of Corporate, Foundation, and Government Grants

Is responsible for prospect research and works cooperatively with school site personnel, volunteers, and grant writers, notifying them of available grants. The position requires grant writing experience, as well as experience in working with corporate, foundation, and government funders.

Director of Major Grants and Gifts

Is responsible for obtaining large grants and gifts from individual donors and will be the key to opening funding doors to angels within your community. The people who make large gifts—more than $10,000—to your cause will bring about positive change within your school or district in the fastest and most significant way. Someone who has extensive experience in both obtaining big gifts and training others to obtain them should fill this key position.

Grant Writers

Depending on your district's size, having one or more full-time, experienced grant writers is essential. In large urban school districts, a cadre of full-time grant writers is needed. A number of people across the country have experience in this area, and you should go after them with gusto. To assist you in recruiting staff, announce these positions in the *Chronicle of Philanthropy*, https://philanthropy.com/ a journal read by most people with experience in the field.

Public schools have many supporters. Millions of people have attended and graduated from schools all across the country. Many of these people have children and grandchildren in the schools and want to give back to show their appreciation and support. While all can't give money or other assets, many can donate time as volunteers. Go after these people with enthusiasm and learn how to ask for their help!

Roles and Responsibilities

As you begin to plan a comprehensive K-12 fundraising effort, it is important that roles and responsibilities be delineated to smoothly transition into this new and exciting adventure. Here is a description for each person or group:

Superintendent

With the board's blessing, the superintendent should be the overall leader in a big-time fundraising effort. This would include, but not be limited to, the establishment of a district-wide development office, including the employment of competent, experienced development office staff. Working with the development staff, as well the local education foundation, central office staff, principals, teachers, parents, volunteers, consultants, and the school board, the superintendent can bring power, prestige, and creativity to the district's overall needs and vision. With training, the superintendent will learn how to ask for gifts from wealthy individuals and others within the school community. A solicitation team—used so effectively by college and university presidents—that includes the superintendent will reap major rewards. Meeting with potential donors personally is the key to money rolling in to your district. Remember, if you don't ask for money, you won't get it.

School Board Members

Individual school board members are key players in a comprehensive district fundraising effort. As such, they should approve the establishment of a development office for the school district and expect it to be a profit center in two years or less. Most board members I know have many friends and contacts in the community and elsewhere, including key people in the business world. Board members should be trained to use these contacts and encouraged to solicit cash and non-cash gifts from friends and colleagues for the schools. And if they can contribute cash or non-cash gifts themselves, why not do so? Board members in the nonprofit world as well as at the private school, college, and university levels contribute regularly to the good causes they represent. It would be wonderfully exciting to see school board members in the public schools set a good example by contributing cash and non-cash gifts to the schools they represent. This good gesture will create a lot of excitement and interest in the community and lead to more gifts. It would also help school board members to solicit monies from others, when they contribute their gift first.

Principals

Principals have critical roles to play as well, and can make or break a fundraising program by their attitude and involvement. Similar to that of the superintendent of schools, principals should be encouraged to make personal visits to wealthy constituents and others in their attendance area to ask for big gifts. This effort should be accomplished as part of a team made up of members of the development office staff, the superintendent, and a board member or two. Principals should also meet personally with program officers and CEOs of corporations and foundations that are interested in funding their specific school.

Teachers, Coaches, and Other Staff

The staff is the heart of the fundraising effort because these are the people on the firing line each and every day. They make the community proud of their involvement and commitment to kids. Band and choir directors, sports and academic coaches, and teachers in both core subjects and the creative and performing arts should be key players. Prospective donors probably know one or more of these people through their kids or grandkids, have been influenced by their good work, and want to help the schools succeed in their fundraising efforts.

Parents and Volunteers

Are important members of the fundraising team and can help reap major rewards in time and money. Most parents want to help the schools, but they are tired of nickel-and-dime fundraising efforts. Many have good contacts in the school community and know where the outside money is. Invite them to assist you in identifying a list of people with money. Make personal visits to prospects along with other members of the solicitation team and encourage parents and volunteers to make contributions as well.

Alumni, Former Public School Staff and People Interested in Helping the Schools

Should take an active role in contributing themselves as well as soliciting grants and gifts from their friends and family. Many of these people would welcome an invitation to give back to the schools by contributing time and money. Invite them into the schools and involve them in your cause. Ask them to assume leadership positions in your foundation. If they contribute large sums of money, consider naming a classroom, a building, or an athletic facility in their honor. It's being done everywhere else. Why not the in the public schools?

DEVELOPMENT OFFICE INFORMATION AND LINKS

http://www.grantsandgiftsforschools.com/ProgramThatPays.pdf

http://www.scholastic.com/browse/article.jsp?id=3746299

http://www.sagepub.com/booksProdDesc.nav?prodId=Book229352

http://www.familycircle.com/teen/school/issues/fundraising/?page=4

https://www.stalbansschool.org/giving/contact-development

HOW TO WORK WITH YOUR BOARD OF TRUSTEES AND YOUR FOUNDATION BOARD

Many school districts have at least two boards. One is the board of trustees, which sets policy for the school district. The other is the board of directors for the district's 501c3 nonprofit foundation or foundations. There are some school districts that don't have a school foundation, but rather work through their P.T.A. or P.T.O. board structure for fundraising. A number of New York City schools raise millions of dollars each year through their P.T.A. board, including Anderson, P.S. 6, P.S. 87, P.S. 234, and P.S. 290. Additionally, there are some districts that have multiple 501c3 foundation boards because there are multiple school foundations within the schools. While this is reality in some places, I would do everything I can to reduce the number of foundations within the schools and district and consolidate to avoid duplication of effort, stepping on each other's toes, and, to enhance coordination and articulation. For large city school districts, I would recommend that you take a look at how boards at nearby colleges and universities are organized. In many universities, there is one overall foundation board that individual schools feed into. The individual schools, such as the School of Education or the School of Law, would have their own 501c3 boards; however, they usually are required to go through the overall foundation board for approval of all grant applications, including budgets and administrative costs. This approach could be adapted for the public schools by allowing each foundation board to be represented on the district 501c3 board.

The boards of directors of 501c3 foundations have the responsibility to ensure that their foundation's mission is carried out and that the foundation has the financial resources to do the job. Board members should be the strongest advocates for the foundation and demonstrate this by not only contributing a generous gift to the organization themselves, but by taking an active role in the overall fundraising effort through devoting adequate time and effort to ensure success. In addition to giving and asking for gifts, board members of 501c3 foundations can assist the staff and the volunteers by making introductions, helping to plan special events, doing prospect research, and becoming personally involved in their areas of interest and expertise. The boards of trustees of school districts have the responsibility of supporting the boards of directors of the 501c3 foundations within their schools and assuring that the foundations are running smoothly and efficiently. In most instances, I recommend that at least one school board member sits on the board of directors of the district's 501c3 foundation to assist with coordination and articulation. I also recommend that some district administrators sit on the 501c3 board.

SOME OF MY CONCERNS

While there are many positive things happening in school and district fundraising at this time, there are also some concerns that continue to persist. They include:

1.   The states and local jurisdictions are not providing enough monies to adequately fund the public schools. More monies need to flow to the schools.

2.   There are too many fundraising groups as well as school foundations competing for the same dollars from the same people. These groups often step on each other's toes related to the raising of outside monies. By consolidating their efforts, this problem will diminish.

In some schools and school districts that are still doing nickel-and-dime fundraising, a tremendous burden is being placed on the parents, kids, and relatives to raise monies regardless of the time and effort it takes. School districts need to take a serious look at this and consider other ways of fundraising. This book is designed to help.

3.   Many foundations as well as P.T.A.s and P.T.O.s in wealthier schools or school districts raise more monies than those in poorer schools and school districts. Board members and others need to figure out ways to equalize funding and access in all schools so that all kids benefit. Of particular concern are kids caught in the middle in schools where they don't receive Federal Title I dollars and the parents don't raise significant dollars. In an attempt to alleviate this problem, California and other states are beginning to make changes in their state funding formulas and are now

funneling additional revenue to schools that serve students with the greatest needs, such as English language learners, children from low-income families, and homeless and foster youth. While these attempts to equalize funding are exceptional, the Portland Public Schools appear to be doing more than most school districts to alleviate some of the above concerns as well as coordinate & articulate their total fundraising effort.

THE FUND FOR PORTLAND PUBLIC SCHOOLS

Recently, the Portland Public Schools started a new non-profit called, The Fund For Public Schools to raise monies from outside funding sources. It will be overseeing 42 local school foundations and have oversight of parent-led fundraising efforts at the school site level beginning July 1, 2019. I mention this school district because it has been at the forefront of education innovation for Pre-K-12 fundraising for years. It appears that they are on the right track for district-wide fundraising efforts including corporate, foundation, government grants, and grants and gifts from individual donors. They also have addressed individual school capacity to give. For example: They want to augment and supplement school site fundraising realizing that some schools cannot raise as much monies as other schools. They also realize that this is not equal education opportunity for all students. As a result, one-third of all funds raised at the school site levels will become part of the Portland Public Schools Parent Fund, which will then contribute monies to schools with less fundraising capacity. I like this concept a lot and hope that it will be implemented in other school districts around the country.

Regardless of the different approaches to Pre-K-12 fundraising being implemented around the country today, it is my belief that additional state and local dollars need to flow to the schools.

There are several very good books written by people with lots of experience on how to be a good board members and how to work with boards. See the links that follow.

BOARDS AND FUNDRAISING BOOKS

The Fundraising Habits of Supremely Successful Boards, by Jerold Panas
> http://emersonandchurch.com/bookstore/the-fundraising-habits-of-supremely-successful-boards/

Fundraising Realities Every Board Member Must Face, by David Lansdowne
> https://www.emersonandchurch.com/products/fundraising-realities-every-board-member-must-face

The Ultimate Board Member's Book, by Kay Sprinkel Grace
> http://emersonandchurch.com/bookstore/the-ultimate-board-members-book/

Chapter 10

Creating and Maintaining School and District 501(c)(3) Foundations

Because the costs of providing a world-class education today go way beyond taxpayer dollars (as it has for state colleges and universities), the public schools have had to pursue outside funding as never before. As such, we are beginning to see school and district 501c3 foundations cropping up all over the country. While this is not an ideal funding situation for the schools, it is reality. Parent and civic groups, chambers of commerce, alumni, booster clubs, and friends of the schools are establishing these foundations in cities, towns, and hamlets across America. In some school districts, school boards have developed their own foundations.

Most schools and school districts are learning the value of having a 501c3 foundation. They know that 501c3s offer tax write-offs for people who give to the schools and also facilitate the acquisition of grants and gifts from corporations and foundations. They understand that this is the way the state colleges and universities are organized and recognize the success that these institutions have had.

There are many estimates as to the numbers of school and district foundations in the United States. My best estimate is that there are approximately 19,000 school and district foundations at this time. Some of these foundations raise little or no money and are difficult to track. Others raise millions! School foundations are growing by leaps and bounds. Many mothers and fathers, grandmothers and grandfathers, alumni and friends, and former teachers and administrators want to give of their time and money to help the schools become first-class learning centers. They know that the schools need their assistance and are willing to put their money on the line to improve their local schools. These people are serious. They want the best for their kids!

FOUR BROAD CATEGORIES OF SCHOOL AND DISTRICT FOUNDATIONS

School-level

These foundations support innovative classroom practices and supplement, augment, and complement programs and activities (such as art, music, physical education, and athletics) not provided for in the budget. Some of these foundations also provide mini-grants for teachers.

Community-based

These independent foundations see themselves as advocates for public education, school improvement, and school reform. They look to broaden the constituency and keep the community informed about the schools' strengths, challenges, and needs.

District-wide

These foundations serve as an arm of the district, just like those at colleges, universities, and private schools. This type of foundation coordinates and facilitates the district's total fundraising effort through a development office with full-time staff and board-approved financial support.

A Combination of Any of the Above

If your school district does not have a 501c3 foundation, it's time to get going. Visit other school or district foundations in your state. Attend meetings, seminars, and webinars to learn how to do it. Develop a website for your foundation. Below are links that will assist you in creating and maintaining 501c3 foundations in your school or district. In addition, there are websites listed to assist you in completing the legal forms necessary, as well as overall information about school and district foundations. For a sampling of 25 foundation websites across the United States, go to the references in Chapter 8.

National School Foundation Association
   http://www.schoolfoundations.org/

National School Board Association
   https://www.nsba.org/

Michigan Association of School Boards
   http://www.masb.org/school-foundations.aspx

Creating Foundations for American Schools, by Dan McCormick
   http://www.amazon.com/Creating-Foundations-For-American-Schools/dp/0834218372

Help Filling Out Your 501(c)(3) Application
   https://form1023.org/

Preparing Your Own 501(c)(3) Application
   https://www.501c3.org/501c3-services/start-a-501c3-nonprofit/

Viewing and Filing Forms 990
    http://nccs.urban.org/

Equalizing Giving to Disadvantaged Schools
    http://greatergood.berkeley.edu/article/item/five_ways_
    to_encourage_giving_to_disadvantaged_public_schools

    http://sfpublicpress.org/news/2014-02/infographics-
    school-fundraising-in-sf-by-the-numbers

Portland Schools to Start New Nonprofit
    http://www.opb.org/news/article/portland-schools-
    new-nonprofit-local-school-foundations/

Chapter 11

Staff Development, Consultant Services and Recruitment

There's a lot of interest around the country in providing staff development and training for teachers, administrators, parents, volunteers, and others related to fundraising. There are also a number of colleges and universities that offer degree and certificate programs. Some corporate and foundation money is available for this purpose. Additionally, a number of consultants and consulting companies are able to assist your school, school district, or foundation with staff development needs in all facets of fundraising. Check the links below and elsewhere.

Recruiting qualified fundraising staff is needed in schools and school districts round the country at this time. The Chronicle of Philanthropy and the Non-Profit Times are very good resources for recruitment of staff from a national pool. There are also consultants that will assist you in your recruitment effort. This could save you time and add expertise to the interview team. Below is a breakdown of links that should help.

STAFF DEVELOPMENT

Lilly Family School of Philanthropy (Indiana University)
http://www.philanthropy.iupui.edu/

Institute for Charitable Giving
http://www.instituteforgiving.org/

Inside Philanthropy
http://www.insidephilanthropy.com/k-12-education/

Nonprofit Solutions
http://www.npsolutions.org/

CONSULTANT SERVICES

Stan Levenson & Associates
http://www.stanlevenson.com

Jerold Panas, Linzy & Partners
http://www.panaslinzy.com/

Jim Collogan
jimcollogan@gmail.com

Elaine Free
http://www.successfulwaysinc.com/

Bill Hoffman & Associates
http://www.billhoffmanandassociates.com/

Jefffrey Lischin
http://www.grantsman.com/

Alexander Haas
http://www.fundraisingcounsel.com/

Grenzebach Glier and Associates (GG+A)
http://www.grenzebachglier.com/education.html

Marts & Lundy
http://www.martsandlundy.com/clients/schools/

Johnson Grossnickle and Associates (JGA)
http://www.jgacounsel.com/

Blackbaud
http://www.blackbaud.com/

Grant Station
https://www.grantstation.com/

National Development Institute (Church Related)
https://nonprofitconferences.org/index.php

RECRUITMENT

The Chronicle of Philanthropy
http://philanthropy.com

http://philanthropy.com/section/
Directory-of-Services/193/

The Non-Profit Times (Resources)
http://www.thenonprofittimes.com/

Chapter 12

Professional Publications

The following links to professional publications are available to you either free or inexpensively. The *Chronicle of Philanthropy* (subscription and online) is read by almost everyone in the field of philanthropy, as well as those looking for a job in philanthropy. Familiarize yourself with the publications on the list, and request those that interest you, your school, and your school district.

Chronicle of Philanthropy
   http://philanthropy.com/section/Home/172

   philanthropy-today@chronicle.com

Inside Philanthropy
   http://www.insidephilanthropy.com/k-12-education/

The NonProfit Times
   http://www.thenonprofittimes.com

Philanthropy Journal
   news@philanthropyjournal.org

Fundraising Success Magazine
   http://www.fundraisingsuccessmag.com/

Future Fundraising Now
http://www.futurefundraisingnow.com/future-fundraising/

Philanthropy News Digest (PND)
http://www.foundationcenter.org/pnd/

Contributions Magazine
http://www.contributionsmagazine.com/about.html

Philanthropy Review
http://www.philanthropy-review.com/

Chapter 13

Professional Associations

There are a number of state associations that are doing a very fine job of providing coordinated services to schools and districts with 501c3 foundations including California, Connecticut, Oklahoma, Florida, and others. However, because the school and district foundation movement in the USA is so young, there are several national associations competing with one another to provide coordinated services to K-12 school and district 501c3 foundations. To have a meaningful national dialogue and to avoid duplication of effort, it is important to unify these national associations into one. Perhaps some of the leaders of state associations might assume the responsibility to do this? For now, it appears that the National School Foundation Association is heading in this direction. It has the name, the interest, and a significant membership. It should also be mentioned that the Association of Fundraising Professionals and the Council for Advancement and Support of Education (CASE) are part of a broader perspective and include colleges, universities, private schools, and nonprofit organizations. See the links that follow.

K-12 ASSOCIATIONS

National School Foundation Association
  http://www.schoolfoundations.org

Grant Professionals Association
  http://grantprofessionals.org/

COLLEGES, UNIVERSITIES, PRIVATE SCHOOLS, AND NONPROFIT ASSOCIATIONS

Association of Fundraising Professionals (AFP)
  http://www.afpnet.org/

Council for Advancement and Support of Education (CASE)
  http://www.case.org/

Chapter 14

Bibliography and Fundraising Blogs

The following bibliography will keep you busy and engaged for a long time. Note that this bibliography is ever changing. Also note that because of space constraints, there are many worthy new books and materials published that have not made it to the list. The Michigan State University Fundraising for Educators Site, prepared by Jon Harrison is one of the most comprehensive available. Take a look at his amazing link below.

It should be mentioned that my multicultural children's book, *Juan and Gwen's Big Fundraising Surprise* has been added to the bibliography and to my knowledge, is the only children's book with a fundraising theme.

There are several fundraising blogs for K-12 at this time; however, most of the blogs are for colleges, universities, and non-profits. Sign up to receive them via e-mail and smart phones. There's much to learn from these blogs.

BIBLIOGRAPHY

Fundraising for Educators, Jon Harrison, Michigan State University
http://staff.lib.msu.edu/harris23/grants/4edfrais.htm

Inside Philanthropy
https://www.insidephilanthropy.com/
fundraising-early-childhood

Emerson & Church Fundraising Books
http://www.contributionsmagazine.com/bookstore.html

http://www.emersonandchurch.com

Wiley Fundraising Books
http://www.wiley.com/WileyCDA/Section/id-
WILEY2_SEARCH_RESULT.html?query=Fundraising

Grant Writing Books on Amazon
http://www.amazon.com/s/ref=nb_sb_
noss_1?url=search-alias%3Dstripbooks&field-
keywords=Grant+Writing+Books

National Center for Charitable Statistics, Urban Institute
http://nccs.urban.org/

Center on Wealth and Philanthropy, Boston College
http://www.bc.edu/research/cwp/

Resources for Nonprofits
http://www.idealist.org/info/Nonprofits

Free Fundraising Management Library
http://managementhelp.org/
nonprofitfundraising/index.htm

Tax Benefits of Giving
http://www.charitynavigator.org/index.
cfm?bay=content.view&cpid=31#.Uw_3Rm_tJ9U

Auctions
https://www.biddingforgood.com/
auction/biddingforgood.action

Some Traditional Fundraising Ideas for Schools
https://hubpages.com/search/?s=Elementary%20
school%20Fundraising

http://www.abcfundraising.com/

http://gafundraising.com/

http://funds2orgs.com/about-us/

CHILDREN'S BOOKS ABOUT FUNDRAISING

*Levenson, Stanley. Juan and Gwen's Big
Fundraising Surprise, 2017. Amazon.*
https://www.amazon.com/Juan-Gwens-
Big-Fundraising-Surprise/dp/0692918167/
ref=cm_cr_arp_d_product_top?ie=UTF8

FUNDRAISING BLOGS

http://www.insidephilanthropy.com/k-12-education/

http://www.aherncomm.com

http://www.fundraisingdetective.
com/fundraising-detective/

http://www.laep.org/blog/

http://101fundraising.org/

http://wildwomanfundraising.com/

http://gettingattention.org/

http://cooldata.wordpress.com/

http://donttellthedonor.blogspot.com/

http://www.gailperry.com/

http://www.frogloop.com/

http://fundraisingcoach.com/

http://www.futurefundraisingnow.com/

http://philanthropy.com/section/Blogs/208/

https://www.networkforgood.com/nonprofitblog/

http://marketingthatworksblog.blogspot.co.nz/

http://www.thefundraisingauthority.com/about/

http://givinginstitute.org/

https://blog.getedfunding.com/

Conclusion

In this revised and updated edition of the book, I have made corrections as needed to the more than 350 available links to enable you to access them with ease and efficiency. I have elaborated and offered suggestions on DonorsChoose.org because it has become so important in the lives of teachers across the USA. I have spent time researching funding agencies for Early Childhood Education because of the importance of early childhood education in the lives of children. I have enhanced the Naming Rights section of the book by adding a number of schools and school districts that have reached out to the community and have become successful in bringing in major dollars in Naming Rights. Their names and accomplishments have been added to this new edition of the book. Also, because so many people have been influenced positively by public school teachers at all levels, I have added a job description for Director of Alumni Relations to the section on Staffing the Development Office. Finally, I talk about The Fund For Portland Public Schools because they come closest to solving the problems that exist today in organizing and articulating Pre-K-12 fundraising.

This revised and updated book, continues to bring you

fresh, new cutting-edge ideas to help close the funding gap that exists in today's Pre-K-12 schools. The ideas presented aren't traditional nickel-and-dime fundraising tactics that are time-consuming and yield minimal results, but rather ideas to direct the flow of money into your classroom, school, foundation, or school district on a continuing basis. The more than 350 updated electronic links included will save you time, energy, and money and will assist you in learning about the latest innovations in fundraising in the USA. Whether you are a classroom teacher, principal, superintendent, school board member, school foundation board member, parent, or a philanthropist, I hope you find this update and revised edition of my book rewarding and that you have learned some things that you have never known before. Good luck to you along the way and please keep in touch via Twitter @StanLevenson

Notes About the Author

Stan Levenson has been involved in K-12 fundraising for more than 45 years. One of the foremost K-12 fundraising writers in America, he is known throughout the world as an author of books and articles on fundraising, as a fundraising guru, as a teacher, and as a storyteller extraordinaire. He has been interviewed on radio and television, online, and in the press, and has been quoted in newspapers and magazines across the nation. He has thousands of followers on Twitter including preK-12 teachers, parents, principals, superintendents, school board members, school foundation board members, and philanthropists. Levenson's fundraising articles have appeared in *The American School Board Journal, Principal Leadership, The School Administrator, Campus Technology*, GetEdFunding, and other publications. He has been quoted on the front page of *USA Today*, as well as in publications including *Scholastic Administrator, Family Circle Magazine, Interactive Educator*, and the *Gotham Gazette*. He holds a B.S. degree from the State University of New York at Oswego; an M.A. degree from U.C.L.A.; and a Ph.D. degree from United States International University (now Alliant International University) in San Diego. Levenson loves to read, write, play tennis, shoot hoops, and travel. He resides in San Diego, California with his wife, Kay Pantelis. You can contact him through Twitter @StanLevenson

Made in the USA
Monee, IL
11 February 2022